TWENTIETH CENTURY VIEWS

The aim of this series is to present the best in contemporary critical opinion on major authors, providing a twentieth century perspective on their changing status in an era of profound revaluation.

Maynard Mack, *Series Editor*
Yale University

DANIEL DEFOE

DANIEL DEFOE

A COLLECTION OF CRITICAL ESSAYS

Edited by

Max Byrd

Prentice-Hall, Inc.
A SPECTRUM BOOK
Englewood Cliffs, N.J.

Library of Congress Cataloging in Publication Data
MAIN ENTRY UNDER TITLE:

Daniel Defoe: a collection of critical essays.

(Twentieth century views) (A Spectrum Book)
Bibliography: p.
1. Defoe, Daniel, 1661?–1731—Addresses, essays,
lectures. I. Byrd, Max.
PR3406.D3   823'.5   75–29297
ISBN 0–13–197608–7
ISBN 0–13–197590–0 pbk.

10   9   8   7   6   5   4   3   2   1

PRENTICE-HALL INTERNATIONAL, INC. *(London)*
PRENTICE-HALL OF AUSTRALIA, PTY. LTD. *(Sydney)*
PRENTICE-HALL OF CANADA, LTD. *(Toronto)*
PRENTICE-HALL OF INDIA PRIVATE LIMITED *(New Delhi)*
PRENTICE-HALL OF JAPAN, INC. *(Tokyo)*
PRENTICE-HALL OF SOUTHEAST ASIA (PTE.) LTD. *(Singapore)*

Contents

DANIEL DEFOE

Introduction

by Max Byrd

In his last surviving portrait Daniel Defoe looks past us with a cold stare. His eyes seem fixed on an object to one side of the frame, the lines of his nostrils and lips are drawn slightly back, one shoulder has pulled taut; he appears somehow tensed, as if he were ready to move away quickly, ready for flight. "I have no doubt he was a precious dry and disagreeable article," Charles Dickens wrote of him unkindly.[1] But it must be confessed that the quality of strain in his portrait tends to bear Dickens out. Defoe looks less like the father of the English novel, the author of *Robinson Crusoe* and *Moll Flanders*, less even like a prosperous London merchant, than what he also was at times: a bankrupt, a political spy, a former inmate of Newgate prison.

His contemporaries had much the same difficulty in seeing him whole. To political and religious enemies he was, as one pamphleteer rather systematically put it, "a Man of great Rashness and Impudence, a mear Mercenary Prostitute, a State Mountebank, an Hackney Tool, a scandalous Pen, a foul-Mouthed Mongrel, an Author who writes for Bread, and lives by Defamation." Others described him as a Proteus, a devil, his throat "a burning Abyss, a Center of Envious Exhalations, set on fire of Hell."[2] Almost everyone agreed that he was sly, scheming, and occasionally hypocritical. Swift, with that wounding indifference he could affect,

[1] Quoted in John Forster, *The Life of Charles Dickens*, ed. J. W. T. Ley (London: Cecil Palmer, 1928), p. 611.

[2] Quoted in Maximillian E. Novak, "Defoe's Use of Irony," in Novak and Herbert J. Davis, *The Uses of Irony* (Los Angeles: Clark Library Papers, 1966), pp. 10–12.

spoke of "the Fellow that was *pilloryed,* I have forgot his Name," and found Defoe "so grave, sententious, dogmatical a rogue that there is no enduring him." [3] To Tory Augustans like Swift and Pope he was a hack journalist in the hire of the Whigs—"Walpole's Laureate"— turning out malicious propaganda to order. To many Whigs he was a polemical and cunning projector, self-righteous to a fault yet apparently not always above shady trading, a liability as often as a spokesman.

But Defoe, like many great writers, has left us in his works a richer, more truthful portrait of himself than any engraving or wrangling contemporary can supply. At the age of fifty-nine, he began an extraordinary burst of creativity that changed the face of English literature: in 1719 *Robinson Crusoe*; in 1720 *Captain Singleton*; in 1722 *Moll Flanders*, *A Journal of the Plague Year*, and *Colonel Jack*; in 1724 *Roxana.* In these novels and in all the detritus of his thirty-odd years of journalism we can draw close to a man whose diversity of interests and whose sustained energy astonish us still: for besides all this, he was a born preacher and gadfly (once intended for the Dissenting ministry) who spun forth plans for economic, social, and political reform as naturally as a spider spins his web; and a versifier, too, whose *True-Born Englishman*, a satirical dressing down of native chauvinism, was the most popular poem of its day. Like all eighteenth-century writers, Defoe was a public and somewhat meddling reformer of his countrymen's lives. Yet none of this remarkable, compulsive activity, as the essays in this volume demonstrate again and again, quite disguises the sensitivity with which he faced in his life and his stories the enduring shocks of human loneliness. If this most prolific of early English writers seems also the most elusive and reserved, that may be in part because the themes of survival and solitude to which he so suddenly turned in 1719 bring us, like him, to the edge of our chairs.

[3] "A Letter Concerning the Sacramental Test," *Prose Works*, ed. Herbert Davis (Oxford: Basil Blackwell, 1940), II, 113. The phrase "Walpole's Laureate" is taken from Ch. VII of Isaac Kramnick, *Bolingbroke and his Circle: The Politics of Nostalgia in the Age of Walpole* (Cambridge, Mass.: Harvard University Press, 1968).

I

It would be interesting to know what finally pushed Defoe to the writing of *Robinson Crusoe*. Hindsight can point to the embryonic novelist in such early self-help works as *The Family Instructor* or in his journal the *Review*, with their scattered snatches of dialogue and narrative. (And *Robinson Crusoe* is a self-help book if ever there was one!) But without some inner act of decision or commitment toward writing a fiction—a thing his Puritan upbringing condemned— Defoe would stand in literary histories only as one more clever forerunner of the English novel, a compatriot of Bunyan and Mrs. Aphra Behn, a shadowy possibility, an "influence" or source. We can only suppose that some deeply personal attraction toward the setting of shipwreck and desert island called forth his resolution. The story of Alexander Selkirk, the sailor marooned four and a half years on an island off the coast of Chile, was certainly the starting point for Defoe. It had, after all, been known in England since 1712; and indeed, Sir Richard Steele had written an account as early as 1713. In the preface to the third part of *Robinson Crusoe*—a collection of essays intended to capitalize on the earlier immense success—Defoe gives us cause to imagine a personal involvement, for there Crusoe declares that "the Story, though Allegorical, is also Historical; and that it is the beautiful Representation of a Life of unexampled Misfortunes, and of a Variety not to be met with in the World, sincerely adapted to, and intended for the common Good of Mankind. . . . Farther, that there is a Man alive, and well known too, the Actions of whose Life are the just Subject of these Volumes, and to whom all or most Part of the Story directly alludes, this may be depended upon for Truth, and to this I set my Name." [4] It is difficult not to hear Defoe's voice over Crusoe's, plaintively reviewing his own checkered career and almost coyly asking to be

[4] *Serious Reflections During the Life and Surprising Adventures of Robinson Crusoe: With his Vision of the Angelick World* (London, 1720), pp. ii–iii.

named. Those suspicions are strengthened by the first of Crusoe's essays, a reflection on "Solitude." Even amid the "greatest Collection of Mankind in the World, I mean, at *London*," Crusoe contends, a man may experience a desirable spiritual solitude, desirable because for a religious man "Life in general is, or ought to be, but one universal Act of Solitude." [5] But the comfort of a holy retreat among multitudes falls away in the face of an absolute reality:

> What are the Sorrows of other Men to us? And what their Joy? Something we may be touch'd indeed with, by the Power of Sympathy, and a secret Turn of the Affections; but all the solid Reflection is directed to our selves. Our Meditations are all Solitude in Perfection; our Passions are all exercised in Retirement; we love, we hate, we covet, we enjoy, all in Privacy and Solitude: All that we communicate of those Things to any other, is but for their Assistance in the Pursuit of our Desires; the End is at Home; the Enjoyment, the Contemplation, is all Solitude and Retirement; 'tis for our selves we enjoy, and for our selves we suffer.[6]

No more appropriate meditation could be found for the shipwrecked Crusoe, but it serves equally well for his creator. We know from many sources how much Defoe regarded himself as mistreated and unlucky, alone in the world and breasting each new wave of misfortune with no help except his own resourcefulness. His terms in prison, perhaps as many as five, for bankruptcy and political misconduct—including the sentence of standing three hours in the pillory at Temple Bar—could only have fanned this sense of persecution. Surely the image of one man struggling as Selkirk did against a hostile wilderness tapped some profound vein of concern for him. Without the central island section, we may say in fact, the rest of *Robinson Crusoe* would take an undistinguished place among all the other adventure narratives of eighteenth-century popular literature; with it, the book enters into the realm of myth, making possible a universal vision of the human condition that must at the same time have sprung from Defoe's vision of himself. Whatever the

[5] Ibid., pp. 4, 2.
[6] Ibid., pp. 2–3.

value of such biographical speculations, however, the immediate result was that, once launched, Defoe rapidly brought forth a whole series of fictional autobiographies that revolve in one fashion or another around these kindred emblems of isolation and renewal.

II

Moll Flanders, said E. M. Forster beautifully, "fills the book that bears her name, or rather stands alone in it, like a tree in a park." [7] But Forster's remark holds true for almost all of Defoe's major books. Generations of readers have commented upon the solitary quality of Defoe's major characters, a quality inherited, so to speak, from Crusoe: Colonel Jack wanders a strangely featureless London terrain virtually alone, recoiling from each encounter with other people to the memorable silences and fears of an orphan childhood; Roxana deliberately breaks off every relationship, sexual or familial, that threatens to bind her; the anonymous narrator of *A Journal of the Plague Year* remains in the stricken city while his brother and friends abandon it. "Crusoe's elaborate self-enclosure," observes George A. Starr, "is only the most graphic version of a task that preoccupies most of Defoe's characters, that of achieving impregnability." [8] And yet the anxieties of impregnability drive them periodically toward relations that are narrowly filial, as Starr notes, a combination of dominant and submissive such as Crusoe and Friday display, but often also simply mercantile, an exchange of services for money such as we see between Colonel Jack and his unnamed banker.

It is this aspect of Defoe's vision, the mercantile, that is perhaps most familiar to us today. The influential criticism of Mark Schorer and Ian Watt in their selections included in this book has gone far toward establishing Defoe, to use Schorer's words, in "the very heart of the middle class." For Schorer, unfortunately, Defoe's

[7] *Aspects of the Novel* (New York: Harcourt, Brace, 1954; first published 1927), p. 88.

[8] Introduction to *Moll Flanders* (London: Oxford University Press, 1971), p. x.

bourgeois limitations are so great, his vision so pinched, that in a book like *Moll Flanders* he records no greater consciousness than the arid "morality of measurement" that we associate with trade. But for Watt a major element in Defoe's appeal is the economic individualism of his characters and the attention he gives to the dignity of their labor; and Crusoe dramatically awakens a pioneering nostalgia as he turns back the clock of modern capitalism, rediscovering all the skills of manufacture and homemaking (like weaving, baking, pottery) now dispersed by technology.

Defoe's picture of "economic man" is most nearly complete in *Robinson Crusoe*, as Watt shows, but his economic concerns break through constantly, and they are neatly emblemized in one of his best-known devices, the elaborate inventories and ledgers that fill all his books. His fiction in particular is lumpy with lengthy entries of lists of stockpiled goods or of sums and losses in business; and these stir contradictory responses in readers, dismissed as padding by some, admired as "verisimilitude" by others. They may serve a deeper novelistic purpose as well: however we regard Defoe's economics, I suspect, we see ourselves reflected in the changing fortunes of his characters; we see our own struggles to tame our balance sheets, and we watch sympathetically over their shoulders as they enter the minutest fluctuations of cash and expenses. There are many possible explanations for the fascination of this bookkeeping process, no doubt—our childish love for certain kinds of busyness, our impulse to quantify—but a powerful aesthetic undercurrent can also be felt in these mundane details. We all have ways to make the flow of time intelligible to ourselves. Their omnipresent account books may serve for Defoe's characters one function that art itself can serve: to organize time and give it meaning. Robinson Crusoe fashions a crude calendar of notches on a stick—for no clear reason—just as prehistoric artists ornamented their tools with diagrams of the cycles of the moon, just as we design our time with divisions of seasons and ceremonies.[9] The narrator of *A Journal of the*

[9] See Alexander Marshack, *The Roots of Civilization* (New York: McGraw-Hill, 1972) for more on this point.

Plague Year searches for the form of disaster in long tallies of deaths and recoveries, parish by parish, week by week, just as the Homeric poems catalogue forests and armies. Moll Flanders to some extent controls her sprawling life and gives it coherence by means of her cashbooks, just as Picasso dated his paintings and as the "numbers" of any poet give cadence to his time, making a dance, or at least a march, of what would otherwise be meaningless movement. More than our bourgeois inclinations draw us to look over their shoulders.

Against these possibilities, however, it must be admitted that Defoe's merchants have their drab dimension and that he does have a tendency to reduce every situation to that of a marketplace. Confronted with the splendid vista of London from a far-off hill in his *Tour thro' the Whole Island of Great Britain*, he pointedly spurns the idealizing portraits of the city that poets like Pope had painted in *Windsor Forest*, a gorgeous metaphorical community of palaces and gardens, and finds his poetry instead in the commercial uses of the serviceable Thames: "As I meet with the River upwards in my Travels thro' the Inland Country, I shall speak of it, as it is the Chanel for conveying an infinite Quantity of Provisions from remote Counties to *London*, and enriching all the Counties again that lye near it, by the return of Wealth and Trade from the City." [10] Even in *A Journal of the Plague Year*, when the city has come to its knees under the impact of an inexplicable fate, the usual meaning of London for Defoe continues to assert itself: a marketplace first, and only incidentally thereafter a center for other human needs and aspirations:

> *John* argu'd very calmly with them a great while, and told them, "That *London* was the Place by which they, that is, the Townsmen of *Epping* and all the Country round them, subsisted; to whom they sold the produce of their Lands, and out of whom they made the Rent of their Farms; and to be so cruel to the Inhabitants of *London* . . . was very hard, . . . when they fled from the Face of the most terrible

[10] Ed. G. D. H. Cole (London: Peter Davies, 1927), I, 174.

Enemy in the World; that it would be enough to make the Name of
an *Epping*-Man hateful thro' all the City, and to have the Rabble
Stone them in the very Streets, whenever they came so much as to
Market." [11]

This orientation toward the market accounts for a good deal of the
disdain Defoe suffered from writers like Swift and Pope, of course,
and Addison and Gay. Defoe's "low" subject matter, his colloquial
prose, his un-classical stress upon commerce ("Writing upon Trade
was the Whore I really doated upon," he confessed in the last
number of his *Review*) all contributed to his exclusion from the
world of politeness to which they belonged. And yet this picture of
Defoe the businessman, Defoe the apologist for the middle classes,
creates an odd contrast to that sense of wounding isolation he
always conveys. It is only when we recall how frequently in his work
trade is identified with crime that the two visions may be
superimposed on one another.

III

In Defoe's fiction the marketplace is a theatre for gentility. There
his characters act out capitalism's reassuring drama of labor and
reward, the conclusion of which is an undramatic bourgeois
security; getting and spending, they lay up their powers. But the
market is by no means a reliable mechanism for these purposes, and
when it falters—when a merchant's commodity fails to sell, as Moll
Flanders' beauty eventually does—its victims literally panic. Colonel Jack's terror over the loss of his gold is a famous instance, but
even a sober handbook like *The Complete English Tradesman* is shot
through with forebodings of bankruptcy, failure, collapse. Collapse,
however, only makes plain what some eighteenth-century writers
had already begun to suspect: the marketplace is as well adapted to
crime as to commerce; Moll can steal as well as sell. In 1705

[11] Ed. Louis A. Landa (London: Oxford University Press, 1969), p. 142.

Bernard de Mandeville scandalized England with a poem called *The Grumbling Hive* (later reworked as *The Fable of the Bees, or Private Vices, Public Benefits*), a homely parable in which the mutual dependence of prosperity and vice was bluntly stated. And John Gay had pointed out the correlation in another way through his reversal of great world and underworld, first in his farce *The Mohocks* and afterwards in *The Beggar's Opera*. Defoe offers no such witty equation of virtue and vice as Mandeville and Gay provide, however, nor anything like their faintly complacent good humor. In Defoe's thought, in fact, although he could write in certain moments that "it must be confess'd, Trade is almost universally founded upon Crime," the two categories are usually kept rigidly separate.[12] His stories make us feel instead the energies of social ambition in constant motion: his heroes rising from poverty to respectability convey to us above all their determination, overriding and instinctual, to rise and stay by any means at hand. It is at this level that crime and the marketplace converge in Defoe's imagination, in the will for survival that all of his characters embody and in the gentility that symbolizes it. But the cost is a heavy one, paid everywhere through his fiction: first, in the fearfulness and instability that both criminal and tradesman must live with; second, in the role of outcast they may be forced to assume. There is in this uncertainty, moreover, the special potential for exile that Defoe seems always alert to, the estrangement implicit in the mechanical, impersonal relationships of ordinary trade, explicit in the disguises and flight that outlawry substitutes for trade. Such an estrangement may be countered for a time by the rhythms of bookkeeping or the comfort of appearances. But sooner or later the love of profit exacts its punishment. And then not only does gentility decay into crime, but the marketplace at last gives way to the prison.

The Justice upon that point committed me, and I was carried to *Newgate;* that horrid Place! my very Blood chills at the mention of its

[12] Quoted in Hans H. Andersen, "The Paradox of Trade and Morality in Defoe" (*Modern Philology*, 39, 1941), p. 28.

Name; the Place, where so many of my Comrades had been lock'd
up, and from whence they went to the fatal Tree; the Place where
my Mother suffered so deeply, where I was brought into the World,
and from whence I expected no Redemption, but by an infamous
Death: To conclude, the Place that had so long expected me, and
which with so much Art and Success I had so long avoided.[13]

Moll's terror at the prospect of Newgate—her "most forcibly urged
emotion," Schorer rather cruelly says—is all the more compelling
in the light of Defoe's other images of it. Prisons, of course, form a
prominent part of the seventeenth-century rogue biographies and
picaresque tales that Defoe often took as models. But the shadow of
Newgate seems to lie ominously along the horizon of all of Defoe's
fiction, literally as in Moll's case and Jack's and Roxana's, or
metaphorically as in the locked houses of *A Journal of the Plague Year*
or Crusoe's island: "my very Heart would die within me, to think of
the Woods, the Mountains, the Desarts I was in; and how I was a
Prisoner lock'd up with the Eternal Bars and Bolts of the Ocean, in
an uninhabited Wilderness, without Redemption." [14] We catch a
note of fatalism in Moll's description of Newgate as "the Place that
had so long expected me," while she fluttered about it like a moth
around a candle; Crusoe too considers his island foreordained by
God, a place that had long expected *him*. Defoe shares his recurrent
image of confinement with a great many other eighteenth-century
writers—we may think of the Happy Valley of Johnson's *Rasselas*,
for example, or the dungeons of every Gothic novel—and its
presence can be understood in one sense as a corrective to the
insistently public character of Augustan literature.[15] But clearly for
Defoe, Newgate prison and all its surrogates symbolize with
paralyzing starkness the theme he first spelled out in Robinson
Crusoe's *Reflections*, the solitude that we are universally doomed to

[13] Starr, *Moll Flanders*, p. 273.

[14] *The Life and Strange Surprizing Adventures of Robinson Crusoe of York, Mariner*
(London: 1719), pp. 132–33.

[15] For more on this topic see my "The Madhouse, the Whorehouse, and the
Convent," *Partisan Review*, forthcoming; and Professor W. B. Carnochan's forthcoming book-length study of the imagery of confinement in the eighteenth century.

suffer. Although they may be swollen to the bursting point with London's miscreants, first among the meanings of Defoe's prisons is the withdrawal from society they entail, their loneliness: Moll's reception by the other inmates is a harsh parody of fellowship; a footprint terrifies Crusoe.

The solitude of such confinement is all the more painful because it comes as punishment either for specific misdeeds, as in Moll's case, or for the more general condition of sinfulness that all of London exhibits to H. F.'s eyes. And yet George A. Starr and others have stressed the extent to which Defoe's novels are based upon Puritan spiritual autobiographies as well as upon the lives of pirates and highwaymen. These models, works like John Bunyan's *Grace Abounding* and Richard Baxter's *Autobiography*, books on which Defoe was reared, tell the story of their authors' sin, repentance, and conversion. And Defoe's characters each follow some version of this course; imprisonment or solitude is only a device that forces them to see their lives steadily for what they are, to repent, and to draw closer to God; it makes possible lasting salvation. "I gave humble and hearty Thanks," Crusoe writes, "that God had been pleas'd to discover to me, even that it was possible I might be more happy in this Solitary Condition, than I should have been in a Liberty of Society, and in all the Pleasures of the World. That he could fully make up to me, the Deficiencies of my Solitary State, and the want of Humane Society by his Presence, and the Communications of his Grace to my Soul." [16] Almost all of Defoe's heroes, as Martin Price says in his contribution to this book, "have a glimpse of some idea of redemption."

It may be objected that salvation for Defoe is no more than a condition of simple security, whether material and middle-class (as in Moll's prosperity) or psychological (as in God's assurance to Crusoe, *"I will never, never leave thee, nor forsake thee"*).[17] And though he protested otherwise, it may be thought that Defoe's incessant

[16] *Robinson Crusoe*, p. 132.
[17] *Robinson Crusoe*, p. 133.

moralizing only masks a disreputable interest in whores and vagabonds; his sincerity, if not his facility, about religion has been doubted from the eighteenth century to the present. But the solitude he envisions for each of us is real enough, and the sense of rescue that repentance and conversion bring is likewise real. Defoe had experienced Newgate at first hand, we remember, just as he had experienced, so he seems to be telling us, the awful solitude of Robinson Crusoe. But we may also surmise from his life that he experienced so lusty a drive for survival that, like Moll Flanders herself, he surrounded and buttressed his central self with disguises, with a novelist's other identities, either to people his solitude or to protect it.

IV

Twentieth-century approaches to Defoe have ranged from the source studies of A. W. Secord to the eloquent impressionistic interpretations of Virginia Woolf and Dorothy Van Ghent. The essays in this volume have been chosen to represent only the high points of the critical range and also to center upon those novels of Defoe's most likely to attract the modern reader: *Robinson Crusoe, Moll Flanders, A Journal of the Plague Year.* It has not been possible to include various important studies of Defoe's journalism or his life, although many scholars, notably James Sutherland and John R. Moore, have labored in these areas with great distinction; Professor Moore in particular has performed the invaluable service of establishing a reliable bibliography.

Recent critical discussion, which occasionally warms up the scholarly presses in a way Defoe might have liked, has revolved around the question of his artfulness. Defoe has often been praised for the "design" of his novels—Coleridge was perhaps the first to celebrate it—and for his conscious control of effect. In *The Rise of the Novel* (1957) Ian Watt, addressing the specific issue of Defoe's irony toward Moll Flanders, argued that, on the contrary, Defoe's craftsmanship is of the most rudimentary and even accidental sort; and he pointed toward Defoe's haste in writing, his simple didactic intentions, his lack both of sophisticated models and of sophistication itself. We are not to project the later history of the novel upon its beginnings, he maintained; we are not to confuse Defoe with Jane Austen or Henry James. For Watt, although there are certainly individual moments of irony in *Moll Flanders*, they "fall far short of the larger, structural irony which would suggest that Defoe viewed either his central character or his purported moral theme ironically." [18] Watt has been challenged by many readers, especially Maximillian E. Novak, who finds Defoe a deliberate, self-conscious stylist. Most of the major statements in the controversy are gathered together in a companion volume to this one, Robert C. Elliott's *Twentieth-Century Interpretations of Moll Flanders*, and in Watt's masterful summary of the criticism since his own book appeared, "The Recent Critical Fortunes of *Moll Flanders*." [19] James Sutherland's remarks on the conclusion of *Roxana* approach the issue of Defoe's craft from biographical and psychological coordinates.

More general surveys are found in Martin Price's essay on Defoe's novels, placing them in the context of themes of energy and order in eighteenth-century literature, and in Benjamin Boyce's discussion of emotion in Defoe's works. Maximillian E. Novak has set out in two books and numerous articles the backgrounds of Defoe's political and philosophic ideas; his rejoinder to another Watt thesis, the view of *Robinson Crusoe* as a typical capitalist entrepreneur, is reprinted here, although the student will want to consult his other works listed in the bibliography. Two other scholars, George A. Starr and J. Paul Hunter, have written extensively about Defoe's religious beliefs, Starr concentrating upon the specific themes and questions that Defoe engages, Hunter more generally upon the role of Puritanism in his imagination; selections

---

[18] *The Rise of the Novel: Studies in Defoe, Richardson and Fielding* (Berkeley and Los Angeles: University of California Press, 1957), p. 122.

[19] *Eighteenth-Century Studies* (1967), I, 109–26.

from their work on *Robinson Crusoe* follow the very different analyses of Virginia Woolf and Novak. Finally, Austin Flanders' essay on *A Journal of the Plague Year* combines sociology and a shrewd critical sense to pry the book loose from antiquarians and topographers and bring it sharply into the modern urban consciousness. Defoe's modernism, of course, may be yet another aspect of his artfulness, and critical battle could be joined next over it. Imlac's observation in *Rasselas* has its application on this point, however, if we are willing to extend it to the beginning of genres: "Whatever be the reason, it is commonly observed that the early writers are in possession of nature, and their followers of art: that the first excel in strength and invention, and the latter in elegance and refinement." [20] Whichever side the reader comes down upon, it is to be hoped that these essays will illuminate once again the wonderful vitality, the "strength and invention" in Johnson's phrase, that Defoe's best novels undeniably possess.

[20] Samuel Johnson, *Rasselas, Poems, and Selected Prose*, ed. Bertrand H. Bronson, 3rd ed. (San Francisco: Rinehart Press, 1971), p. 627.

Defoe

by Virginia Woolf

The fear which attacks the recorder of centenaries lest he should find himself measuring a diminishing spectre and forced to foretell its approaching dissolution is not only absent in the case of *Robinson Crusoe* but the mere thought of it is ridiculous. It may be true that *Robinson Crusoe* is two hundred years of age upon the twenty-fifth of April 1919, but far from raising the familiar speculations as to whether people now read it and will continue to read it, the effect of the bicentenary is to make us marvel that *Robinson Crusoe*, the perennial and immortal, should have been in existence so short a time as that. The book resembles one of the anonymous productions of the race rather than the effort of a single mind; and as for celebrating its centenary we should as soon think of celebrating the centenaries of Stonehenge itself. Something of this we may attribute to the fact that we have all had *Robinson Crusoe* read aloud to us as children, and were thus much in the same state of mind towards Defoe and his story that the Greeks were in towards Homer. It never occurred to us that there was such a person as Defoe, and to have been told that *Robinson Crusoe* was the work of a man with a pen in his hand would either have disturbed us unpleasantly or meant nothing at all. The impressions of childhood are those that last longest and cut deepest. It still seems that the name of Daniel Defoe has no right to appear upon the title-page of *Robinson Crusoe*, and if we celebrate the bicentenary of the book we are making a slightly unnecessary allusion to the fact that, like Stonehenge, it is still in existence.

The great fame of the book has done its author some injustice; for while it has given him a kind of anonymous glory it has obscured the fact that he was a writer of other works which, it is safe to assert, were not read aloud to us as children. Thus when the Editor of the *Christian World* in the year 1870 appealed to "the boys and girls of England" to erect a monument upon the grave of Defoe, which a stroke of lightning had mutilated, the marble was inscribed to the memory of the author of *Robinson Crusoe*. No mention was made of *Moll Flanders*. Considering the topics which are dealt with in that book, and in *Roxana, Captain Singleton, Colonel Jack* and the rest, we need not be surprised, though we may be indignant, at the omission. We may agree with Mr. Wright, the biographer of Defoe, that these "are not works for the drawing-room table." But unless we consent to make that useful piece of furniture the final arbiter of taste, we must deplore the fact that their superficial coarseness, or the universal celebrity of *Robinson Crusoe*, has led them to be far less widely famed than they deserve. On any monument worthy of the name of monument the names of *Moll Flanders* and *Roxana*, at least, should be carved as deeply as the name of Defoe. They stand among the few English novels which we can call indisputably great. The occasion of the bicentenary of their more famous companion may well lead us to consider in what their greatness, which has so much in common with his, may be found to consist.

Defoe was an elderly man when he turned novelist, many years the predecessor of Richardson and Fielding, and one of the first indeed to shape the novel and launch it on its way. But it is unnecessary to labour the fact of his precedence, except that he came to his novel-writing with certain conceptions about the art which he derived partly from being himself one of the first to practise it. The novel had to justify its existence by telling a true story and preaching a sound moral. "This supplying a story by invention is certainly a most scandalous crime," he wrote. "It is a sort of lying that makes a great hole in the heart, in which by degrees a habit of lying enters in." Either in the preface or in the text of each of his works, therefore, he takes pains to insist that he has not used his invention at all but has depended upon facts, and that his purpose has been the highly moral desire to convert the vicious or to warn the innocent. Happily these were principles that tallied very well with his natural disposition and endowments. Facts had been drilled into him by sixty years of varying fortunes before he turned his experience to account in fiction. "I have some time ago summed up the Scenes of my life in this distich," he wrote:

> No man has tasted differing fortunes more,
> And thirteen times I have been rich and poor.

He had spent eighteen months in Newgate and talked with thieves, pirates, highwaymen, and coiners before he wrote the history of Moll Flanders. But to have facts thrust upon you by dint of living and accident is one thing; to swallow them voraciously and retain the imprint of them indelibly, is another. It is not merely that Defoe knew the stress of poverty and had talked with the victims of it, but that the unsheltered life, exposed to circumstances and forced to shift for itself, appealed to him imaginatively as the right matter for his art. In the first pages of each of his great novels he reduces his hero or heroine to such a state of unfriended misery that their existence must be a continued struggle, and their survival at all the result of luck and their own exertions. Moll Flanders was born in Newgate of a criminal mother; Captain Singleton was stolen as a child and sold to the gipsies; Colonel Jack, though "born a gentleman, was put 'prentice to a pick-pocket"; Roxana starts under better auspices, but, having married at fifteen, she sees her husband go bankrupt and is left with five children in "a condition the most deplorable that words can express."

Thus each of these boys and girls has the world to begin and the battle to fight for himself. The situation thus created was entirely to Defoe's liking. From her very birth or with half a year's respite at most, Moll Flanders, the most notable of them, is goaded by "that worst of devils, poverty," forced to earn her living as soon as she can sew, driven from place to place, making no demands upon her creator for the subtle domestic atmosphere which he was unable to supply, but drawing upon him for all he knew of strange people and customs. From the outset the burden of proving her right to exist is laid upon her. She has to depend entirely upon her own wits and judgement, and to deal with each emergency as it arises by a rule-of-thumb morality which she has forged in her own head. The briskness of the story is due partly to the fact that having transgressed the accepted laws at a very early age she has henceforth the freedom of the outcast. The one impossible event is that she should settle down in comfort and security. But from the first the peculiar genius of the author asserts itself, and avoids the obvious danger of the novel of adventure. He makes us understand that Moll Flanders was a woman on her own account and not only material for a succession of adventures. In proof of this she begins, as Roxana also begins, by falling passionately, if unfortunately, in love. That she must rouse herself and marry some one else and look very closely to her settlements and prospects is no slight upon her passion, but to be laid to the charge of her birth; and, like all Defoe's women, she is a person of robust understanding. Since she makes no scruple of telling lies when they serve her purpose, there is something undeniable about her truth when she speaks it. She has no time to waste upon the refinements of personal affection; one tear is dropped, one moment of despair allowed, and then "on with the story." She has a spirit that loves to breast the storm. She delights in the exercise of her own powers. When she discovers that the man she has married in Virginia is her own brother she is violently disgusted; she insists upon leaving him; but as soon as she sets foot in Bristol, "I took the diversion of going to Bath, for as I was still far from being old so my humour, which was always gay, continued so to an extreme." Heartless she is not, nor can any one charge her with levity; but life delights her, and a heroine who lives has us all in tow. Moreover, her ambition has that slight strain of imagination in it which puts it in the category of the noble passions. Shrewd and practical of necessity, she is yet haunted by a desire for

romance and for the quality which to her perception makes a man
a gentleman. "It was really a true gallant spirit he was of, and it
was the more grievous to me. 'Tis something of relief even to be
undone by a man of honour rather than by a scoundrel," she writes
when she had misled a highwayman as to the extent of her fortune.
It is in keeping with this temper that she should be proud of her
final partner because he refuses to work when they reach the
plantations but prefers hunting, and that she should take pleasure
in buying him wigs and silver-hilted swords "to make him appear,
as he really was, a very fine gentleman." Her very love of hot
weather is in keeping, and the passion with which she kissed the
ground that her son had trod on, and her noble tolerance of every
kind of fault so long as it is not "complete baseness of spirit,
imperious, cruel, and relentless when uppermost, abject and
low-spirited when down." For the rest of the world she has nothing
but good-will.

Since the list of the qualities and graces of this seasoned old
sinner is by no means exhausted we can well understand how it was
that Borrow's apple-woman on London Bridge called her "blessed
Mary" and valued her book above all the apples on her stall; and
that Borrow, taking the book deep into the booth, read till his eyes
ached. But we dwell upon such signs of character only by way of
proof that the creator of Moll Flanders was not, as he has been
accused of being, a mere journalist and literal recorder of facts with
no conception of the nature of psychology. It is true that his
characters take shape and substance of their own accord, as if in
despite of the author and not altogether to his liking. He never
lingers or stresses any point of subtlety or pathos, but presses on
imperturbably as if they came there without his knowledge. A touch
of imagination, such as that when the Prince sits by his son's cradle
and Roxana observes how "he loved to look at it when it was
asleep," seems to mean much more to us than to him. After the
curiously modern dissertation upon the need of communicating
matters of importance to a second person lest, like the thief in
Newgate, we should talk of it in our sleep, he apologises for his

digression. He seems to have taken his characters so deeply into his mind that he lived them without exactly knowing how; and, like all unconscious artists, he leaves more gold in his work than his own generation was able to bring to the surface.

The interpretation that we put on his characters might therefore well have puzzled him. We find for ourselves meanings which he was careful to disguise even from his own eye. Thus it comes about that we admire Moll Flanders far more than we blame her. Nor can we believe that Defoe had made up his mind as to the precise degree of her guilt, or was unaware that in considering the lives of the abandoned he raised many deep questions and hinted, if he did not state, answers quite at variance with his professions of belief. From the evidence supplied by his essay upon the "Education of Women" we know that he had thought deeply and much in advance of his age upon the capacities of women, which he rated very high, and the injustice done to them, which he rated very harsh.

> I have often thought of it as one of the most barbarous customs in the world, considering us as a civilised and a Christian country, that we deny the advantages of learning to women. We reproach the sex every day with folly and impertinence; which I am confident, had they the advantages of education equal to us, they would be guilty of less than ourselves.

The advocates of women's rights would hardly care, perhaps, to claim Moll Flanders and Roxana among their patron saints; and yet it is clear that Defoe not only intended them to speak some very modern doctrines upon the subject, but placed them in circumstances where their peculiar hardships are displayed in such a way as to elicit our sympathy. Courage, said Moll Flanders, was what women needed, and the power to "stand their ground"; and at once gave practical demonstration of the benefits that would result. Roxana, a lady of the same profession, argues more subtly against the slavery of marriage. She "had started a new thing in the world" the merchant told her; "it was a way of arguing contrary to the general practise." But Defoe is the last writer to be guilty of bald preaching. Roxana keeps our attention because she is blessedly unconscious that she is in any good sense an example to her sex and is thus at liberty to own that part of her argument is "of an elevated strain which was really not in my thoughts at first, at all." The knowledge of her own frailties and the honest questioning of her own motives, which that knowledge begets, have the happy result of keeping her fresh and human when the martyrs and pioneers of so many problem novels have shrunken and shrivelled to the pegs and props of their respective creeds.

But the claim of Defoe upon our admiration does not rest upon the fact that he can be shown to have anticipated some of the views of Meredith, or to have written scenes which (the odd suggestion occurs) might have been turned into plays by Ibsen. Whatever his ideas upon the position of women, they are an incidental result of his chief virtue, which is that he deals with the important and lasting side of things and not with the passing and trivial. He is often dull. He can imitate the matter-of-fact precision of a scientific traveller until we wonder that his pen could trace or his brain conceive what has not even the excuse of truth to soften its dryness. He leaves out the whole of vegetable nature, and a large part of human nature. All this we may admit, though we have to admit defects as grave in many writers whom we call great. But that does not impair the peculiar merit of what remains. Having at the outset limited his scope and confined his ambitions he achieves a truth of insight which is far rarer and more enduring than the truth of fact which he professed to make his aim. Moll Flanders and her friends recommended themselves to him not because they were, as we should say, "picturesque"; nor, as he affirmed, because they were examples of evil living by which the public might profit. It was their natural veracity, bred in them by a life of hardship, that excited his interest. For them there were no excuses; no kindly shelter obscured their motives. Poverty was their taskmaster. Defoe did not pronounce more than a judgement of the lips upon their failings. But their courage and resource and tenacity delighted him. He found their society full of good talk, and pleasant stories, and faith in each other, and morality of a home-made kind. Their fortunes had that infinite variety which he praised and relished and beheld with wonder in his own life. These men and women, above all, were free to talk openly of the passions and desires which have moved men and women since the beginning of time, and thus even now they keep their vitality undiminished. There is a dignity in everything that is looked at openly. Even the sordid subject of money, which plays so large a part in their histories, becomes not sordid but tragic when it stands not for ease and consequence but for honour, honesty, and life itself. You may object that Defoe is humdrum, but never that he is engrossed with petty things.

He belongs, indeed, to the school of the great plain writers, whose work is founded upon a knowledge of what is most persistent, though not most seductive, in human nature. The view of London from Hungerford Bridge, grey, serious, massive, and full of the subdued stir of traffic and business, prosaic if it were not for the masts of the ships and the towers and domes of the city, brings him to mind. The tattered girls with violets in their hands at the street corners, and the old weather-beaten women patiently displaying their matches and boot-laces beneath the shelter of arches, seem like characters from his books. He is of the school of Crabbe and of Gissing, and not merely a fellow-pupil in the same stern place of learning, but its founder and master.

Defoe's Novels

by Martin Price

The rise of the novel in the eighteenth century is the triumph of the particular, however we may explain the novel's coming into being. Two major tendencies feed into the central event. The mock heroic of Cervantes and his followers subjects the heroic image to the punishing presence of the commonplace. And the marvelous is naturalized as the saint's life, the rogue's picaresque career, the pilgrimage of the individual soul, are all enmeshed in the business of daily existence. The heroic may survive its punishment, but it takes on a new form. The allegorical translucency of the saint's life or of the pilgrim's progress may survive to some extent, but saint and pilgrim alike have now become first of all people with familiar names and addresses, with aunts and cousins, and the elaborate costume of a social existence. Saints become Clarissa Harlowes; pilgrims become Robinson Crusoes; and rogues become—instead of the resilient heroes of a hundred escapades—characters disclosed in the long, disorderly memoirs of Moll Flanders.

The triumph of the particular is the triumph of formal realism, a realism used to a different degree and for a different end by each of the great novelists of the century. The novel provides a spacious vehicle, with its slow rhythm of disclosure, its opportunities for dialogue, description, commentary. None of these is new in itself. They appear in epic, in romance, and in the genres of drama—but the mixture is new. The novel allows a rapid alternation between

"Defoe's Novels." From "The Divided Heart" in *To the Palace of Wisdom: Studies in Order and Energy from Dryden to Blake*, by Martin Price (Garden City, N.Y.: Doubleday & Company, Inc., 1964), pp. 263–76. Reprinted by permission.

the character's internal thought and his action; between his view of himself and the author's view of him; between the intense scrutiny and the panoramic view. The novel gains fluidity by its prosiness. It sacrifices the concentration of poetic language for a new fusion of the poetic and the documentary, and for a more thoroughgoing involvement of the significant in the circumstances where it must find its life and from which it must wrest its values. The novel is the medium in which we can see the spirit of man in its most problematic form—not in lucid contests of principle but (in Lionel Trilling's words) "as it exists in the inescapable conditions which the actual and the trivial make for it" (*The Opposing Self*, New York, 1955, p. 75).

Defoe's novels—written late in a career given over to journalism and pamphleteering—have always been a puzzle to the critic. Defoe draws upon forms of autobiography as far apart as criminals' sensational narratives of their careers and Puritan preachers' records of their transactions with God and the devil, factual narratives of sea discoveries, and pious accounts of miraculous providences. Running through this compound is the troubled conscience of a Puritan tradesman, aware of the frequent conflict between the demands of commercial gain and those of spiritual salvation. It is this troubled conscience that gives his characters their depth. They are tremendously efficient and resourceful in meeting the difficulties of their "trade," and Defoe catches the excitement of their limited but genuine art. But they are also nagged by doubt and a sense of guilt, by an awareness of what they have ignored or put by in their single-minded commitment. These pangs are not, in most cases, very effectual, but they are none the less authentic. Defoe's characters participate, as often as not, in what Iris Murdoch calls the "dialectic of those who habitually succumb to temptation."

In the novels I shall consider Defoe gives us the great myth of the isolated man bringing order out of unfamiliar materials (the first part of *Robinson Crusoe*), the outlawry of a woman whose social isolation makes her a freebooter in the center of London (*Moll*

Flanders), and the recovery of a man from the life of crime into which he is plunged as a child *(Colonel Jack)*.[1] All these characters aspire to some kind of morality; all have a glimpse of some idea of redemption. Without these aspirations, they would be near successors to the picaresque heroes of countless jestbooks, coming through dangerous scrapes with wily dexterity. If the aspirations had fuller control of their natures, they might become the heirs of those spiritual heroes who find their way at last from the City of Destruction to the Land of Beulah. But their lives remain curiously unresolved and open. As Ian Watt has said, "Defoe presents us with a narrative in which both 'high' and 'low' motives are treated with equal seriousness: the moral continuum of his novels is much closer than was that of any previous fiction to the complex combination of spiritual and material issues which moral choices in daily life customarily involve" (*The Rise of the Novel*, p. 83).

Defoe remains a puzzle because he imposes little thematic unity on his materials. Usually the writer who is content to give us the shape of the tale itself has a shapely tale to tell; a tale with its own logic, its awakening of tensions and expectations, its mounting repetition, its elaborate devices for forestalling too direct a resolution, and its satisfying—perhaps ingeniously surprising—way of tying all its threads in one great stroke. Such a tale need not leave those gaps in its narrative that are occasions for us to consider its meaning or theme. In Defoe's narratives the inconsistencies are such that we want to find a significant design, yet they hardly accommodate our wish.

Some critics have found consistent irony in a work like *Moll Flanders* by trimming away troublesome details, hardening the central character, and importing a moral stridency Defoe does not invite. Dorothy Van Ghent finds in Moll "the immense and seminal reality of an Earth Mother, progenitrix of the wasteland, sower of our harvests of technological skill, bombs, gadgets, and the plati-

---

[1] For the text of Defoe, I have given volume and page references to *Romances and Narratives of Daniel Defoe*, ed. George A. Aitken, London, 1895.

tudes and stereotypes and absurdities of a morality suitable to a wasteland world." This seems to me at once a great deal more fastidious and more vehement than the attitudes that underlie Defoe's conception of his heroine. The fact that Moll measures her success by money does not necessarily mean that money is her only object. Nor does Moll's indifference to the sensuousness and concrete texture of experience make her "monstrously abnormal" (*The English Novel: Form and Function*, New York, 1953, p. 43).

Moll Flanders is the chronicle of a full life-span, told by a woman in her seventieth year with wonder and acceptance. In one sense, she is the product of a Puritan society turned to worldly zeal. Hers is very much the world of the Peachums, and in it Moll is the supreme tradeswoman, always ready to draw up an account, to enter each experience in her ledger as profit or loss, bustling with incredible force in the market place of marriage, and finally turning to those bolder and franker forms of competitive enterprise, whoredom and theft. To an extent, she is the embodiment of thrift, good management, and industry. But she is also the perverse and savagely acquisitive outlaw, the once-dedicated servant of the Lord turned to the false worship of wealth, power, success.

Her drive is in part the inevitable quest for security, the island of property that will keep one above the waters of an individualistic, cruelly commercial society. Born in Newgate, left with no resources but her needle, she constantly seeks enough wealth or a wealthy enough husband to free her from the threat of poverty and the temptations of crime. But she finds herself fascinated by the quest itself, by the management of marriages, the danger of thievery. When she has more money than she needs, she is still disguising herself for new crimes, disdaining the humble trade of the seamstress. When she finally settles into respectability, it is with a gentleman, not a merchant; her husband is a rather pretentious, somewhat sentimental highwayman, who is not much good as a farmer but is a considerable sportsman. Moll is no simple middle-class mercantile figure; nor is she another Macheath. Yet she has elements of both.

There is still another dimension of Moll Flanders. Her constant moral resolutions, her efforts to reform, her doubts and remorse cannot be discounted as hypocrisy or even unrealistic self-deception. Moll is a daughter of Puritan thought, and her piety has all the troublesome ambiguities of the Puritan faith. Her religion and morality are not the rational and calculating hypocrisy of the simple canter—the Shimei of Dryden's *Absalom and Achitophel*, for example. They are essentially emotional. She has scruples against incest, but they take the form of nausea, physical revulsion. She intends virtuous behavior and is astonished to discover her hardness of heart. Moll's life is a career of self-discovery, of "herself surprised," surprised by herself and with herself. Just as for the earlier Puritan, the coming of grace might be unpredictable, terrifyingly sudden, and very possibly deceptive, so for Moll the ways of her heart are revealed to her by her conduct more than by her consciousness, and even her most earnest repentance arouses her own distrust until it can well up into an uncontrollable joy. Personality is not something created or earned; the self is not the stable essence the Stoic moralist might seek. It is something given, whether by God or the devil, always in process, eluding definition and slipping away from rational purpose. Even at her happiest, with the man she has long missed, and in the late autumn of her life, Moll can think of how pleasant life might still be without him. It is a wayward thought, a momentary inclination, as real as her devotion and no more real.

What we find in Moll Flanders is not an object lesson in Puritan avarice or in the misuse of divinely given talents. Moll has all the confusion of a life torn between worldliness and devotion, but what remains constant is the energy of life itself, the exuberant innocence that never learns from experience and meets each new event with surprise and force. Moll, like the secularized Puritanism she bespeaks, has the zeal that might found sects as well as amass booty, that might colonize a new world as readily as it robbed an old one. And the form of the old zeal, now turned into a secular world, needing the old faith at least intermittently as the new devotion to the world falters with failure, gives us a pattern of character that is one of the remarkable creations of fiction. Defoe, we are told, seems not to judge his material; Defoe must be a brilliant ironist. Both assertions imply a set of values thinner and more neatly ordered than Defoe can offer. He is aware of the tension between the adventurous spirit and the old piety; he can see the vitality of both religious zeal and worldly industry; the thrifty efficiency and the reckless outlawry that are both aspects of the middle-class adventure; the wonderful excitement of technology as well as its darker omens. And seeing all of this, he does not seem to see the need to reduce these tensions to a moral judgment. Like Mandeville, who struts much more in the role, he is one of the artists who make our moral judgments more difficult.

Ultimately, one might call Defoe a comic artist. The structure of *Moll Flanders* itself defies resolution. In giving us the life-span, with its eager thrust from one experience to the next, Defoe robs life of its climactic structure. Does Moll face marriage to the brother of her seducer, a seducer she still loves? It is an impossible tragic dilemma. Yet the marriage takes place, the husband dies, the children are placed; and Moll is left taking stock as she enters the marriage market again. Does she face the dreadful fact of incest? This, too, passes away; she cannot reconcile herself to it, but she can make a settlement and depart in search of a new and illegal marriage. The commonplace inevitably recurs; we have parodies of tragic situations.

Moll herself is not contemptible in her insensitivity. She is magnificently unheroic; and yet there is a modest touch of heroism in her power of recuperation, her capacity for survival with decency. In her curiously meaningless life, there is a wonderful intensity of experience at a level where affection, inclination, impulse (both generous and cruel) generate all the motions that are usually governed, or perhaps simply accompanied, by a world of thought. We have Defoe's own account of this process in his *Serious Reflections of Robinson Crusoe* (iv):

> There is an inconsiderate temper which reigns in our minds, that
> hurries us down the stream of our affections by a kind of involuntary

agency, and makes us do a thousand things, in the doing of which we propose nothing to ourselves but an immediate subjection to our will, that is to say, our passion, even without the concurrence of our understandings, and of which we can give very little account after 'tis done.

This way of reading *Moll Flanders* imposes its own straitening on the untidy fullness of the book. Ian Watt has made a decisive case for the comparative artlessness of Defoe; there are too many wasted emphases, too many simple deficiencies of realization to make the case for deliberate irony tenable. But one can claim for Defoe a sensibility that admits more than it can fully articulate, that is particularly alert to unresolved paradoxes in human behavior. Watt dismisses in passing the parallel of a work like Joyce Cary's *Herself Surprised.* There is point in this dismissal, for Cary has raised to clear thematic emphasis what is left more reticent in Defoe. Yet the relationship is worth exploration. Few writers have been so fascinated as Cary with the ambiguities of the protestant temper. In a great many characters—among them the statesman, Chester Nimmo, in the political trilogy and the evangelical faith-healer Preedy in the last novel, *The Captive and the Free*—Cary studied the shimmering iridescence with which motives seem, from different angles, dedicated service and the search for grace or the most opportunistic self-seeking. Cary was not interested in "rationalization" but in the peculiar power achieved by the coincidence of religious zeal and imperious egoism. Preedy, for example, seduces a young girl and makes her virtually his slave; but he is convinced that his power to win her love is a sign of grace—that a love so undemanding and undeserved as hers can only be a sign of God's love in turn. Preedy is monstrous in one aspect, terrifying but comprehensible in another; the difference lies in what we recognize to be his object.

Cary's effects are so adroit and so carefully repeated that we have no doubt about calling them ironic. Defoe's are less artful and less completely the point of his tale. Yet his awareness of them seems no less genuine. Defoe's characters have secularized old Puritan modes of thought. Moll Flanders is constantly taking inventory and casting up her accounts as she faces a new stage of her life. Crusoe, too, keeps an account book, and, more like the earlier Puritans, an account book of the soul. The doctrine of regeneration, we are told, caused the Puritans "to become experts in psychological dissection and connoisseurs of moods before it made them moralists. It forced them into solitude and meditation by requiring them continually to cast up their accounts." [2] In the diary, particularly, the Puritan might weigh each night what he had experienced of God's deliverance or of Satan's temptation during the day. "It was of the very essence of Puritan self-discipline that whatsoever thoughts and actions the old Adam within had most desire to keep hidden, the very worst abominations of the heart, one must when one retired to one's private chamber at night draw into the light of conscience. . . . Having thus balanced his spiritual books, he could go to bed with a good conscience, sleep sound and wake with courage." [3]

The "other-worldliness" of Puritan theology was, as Perry Miller puts it, "a recognition of the world, an awareness of a trait in human nature, a witness to the devious ways in which men can pervert the fruits of the earth and the creatures of the world and cause them to minister to their vices. Puritanism found the natural man invariably running into excess or intemperance, and saw in such abuses an affront to God, who had made all things to be used according to their natures. Puritanism condemned not natural passions but inordinate passions" (p. 42).

This concern with the uses of things places emphasis not on their sensuous fullness but on their moral function, and the seeming bleakness of Defoe's world of measurables derives in part from this. Characteristically, when Defoe in his *Tour* praises the countryside, it is for what man has made of it: "nothing can be more beautiful; here is a plain and pleasant country, a rich fertile soil, cultivated and enclosed to the utmost perfection of husbandry, then bespan-

[2] Perry Miller, *The New England Mind*, New York, 1939, p. 53.
[3] William Haller, *The Rise of Puritanism*, New York, 1938, pp. 99–100.

gled with villages; those villages filled with these houses, and the houses surrounded with gardens, walks, vistas, avenues, representing all the beauties of buildings, and all the pleasures of planting. . . ." So, too, the natural scene of Crusoe's island "appeals not for adoration, but for exploitation" (Ian Watt, p. 70). It is not the things we care about but the motives or energies they bring into play: they may satisfy needs, or call forth technical ingenuity, or present temptations. The physical reality of sensual temptation need not be dwelt upon, for moral obliviousness or self-deception is Defoe's concern (as in the account of Moll's going to bed with the Bath gentleman). If Moll's inventories seem gross, they may also be seen as the balance of freedom against necessity; poverty is the inescapable temptation to crime. And her inventories are, in an oblique sense, still account books of the spirit.

What might once have served the cause of piety becomes a temptation to exploitation. This is the dialectic of which Perry Miller speaks: the natural passion insensibly turns into the inordinate passion. Each of Defoe's central characters at some point passes the boundary between need and acquisitiveness, between the search for subsistence and the love of outlawry. And it is only in the coolness of retrospect that they can see the transgression. Defoe does not play satirically upon their defections; he knows these to be inevitable, terrifying so long as they can be seen with moral clarity, but hard to keep in such clear focus. His characters live in a moral twilight, and this leads to Defoe as a writer of comedy.

We must also keep in mind the essential optimism of the Puritan creed. The Puritans could not, Perry Miller tells us, sustain the tragic sense of life. "They remembered their cosmic optimism in the midst of anguish, and they were too busy waging war against sin, too intoxicated with the exultation of the conflict to find occasional reversals, however costly, any cause for deep discouragement. . . . Far from making for tragedy, the necessity [for battle] produced exhilaration" (p. 37). The battle against sin is not, of course, the only battle in which Defoe's characters are involved, but the struggle in the world demands the same intense concentration and

affords the same exhilaration. If there is any central motive in
Defoe's novels, it is the pleasure in technical mastery: the fascination with how things get done, how Crusoe makes an earthenware
pot or Moll Flanders dexterously makes off with a watch. The
intensity of this concentration gives an almost allegorical cast to the
operation, as if Crusoe's craftsmanship had the urgency of the art
by which a man shapes his own soul. It is beside the point to
complain that these operations are "merely" technical and practical; undoubtedly the man who invented the wheel had beside him a
high-minded friend who reproached him with profaning the
mystery of the circle by putting it to such menial uses. The delight
in mastery and in problem-solving may be a lower and less liberal
art than those we commonly admire, but it is a fundamental
experience of men and a precious one.

Even more, the energy of spirit that is concentrated in these
operations is a source of joy. One might wish that Moll Flanders
had founded a garden suburb with the force she gave to robbing a
child, and at moments she feels so too; but the strength she brings to
the demands of life is at worst a perversion of the spiritual energy
the Puritan seeks to keep alive. It is in doing that he finds himself
and serves himself, and Moll Flanders reaches the lowest point of
her life when she falls into the apathy of despair in Newgate: "I
degenerated into stone, I turned first stupid and senseless, then
brutish and thoughtless, and at last raving mad as any of them
were; in short, I became as naturally pleased and easy with the
place as if indeed I had been born there." She loses her sense of
remorse:

> a certain strange lethargy of soul possessed me; I had no trouble, no
> apprehensions, no sorrow about me, the first surprise was gone. . . .
> my senses, my reason, nay, my conscience, were all asleep . . . (VIII,
> 94).

In contrast is the recovered energy that comes with her repentance:

> I was covered with shame and tears for things past, and yet had at
> the same time a secret surprising joy at the prospect of being a true

penitent . . . and so swift did thought circulate, and so high did the impressions they had made upon me run, that I thought I could freely have gone out that minute to execution, without any uneasiness at all, casting my soul entirely into the arms of infinite mercy as a penitent (VIII, 105).

These moments of spiritual despair and joy have their counterparts in her secular life as well. After the death of her honest husband, she is left in poverty:

I lived two years in this dismal condition, wasting that little I had, weeping continually over my dismal circumstances, and as it were only bleeding to death, without the least hope or prospect of help . . . (VII, 199).

With the pressure of poverty and the temptation of the Devil, she commits her first theft and runs through a tortured circuit of streets:

I felt not the ground I stepped on, and the farther I was out of danger, the faster I went. . . . I rested me a little and went on; my blood was all in a fire, my heart beat as if I was in a sudden fright: in short, I was under such a surprise that I knew not whither I was going, or what to do (VII, 201).

This is the energy of fear, but it is a return to life; and before many pages have passed, Moll is speaking with pleasure of her new art.

The benign form of this energy is that of the honest tradesman whom Defoe always celebrates: "full of vigor, full of vitality, always striving and bustling, never idle, never sottish; his head and his heart are employed; he moves with a kind of velocity unknown to other men" (*Complete English Tradesman*, II [1727], i, 106–7). As R. H. Tawney has written, "a creed which transformed the acquisition of wealth from a drudgery or a temptation into a moral duty was the milk of lions" (*Religion and the Rise of Capitalism*, London, 1926, ch. IV, iii). Yet, as Tawney recognizes, the older Puritan view of the evil of inordinate desires still survived. Defoe may call gain "the tradesman's life, the essence of his being" (*CET*, II, i, 79–80), but gain makes it all the harder for a tradesman to be an honest man: "There are more snares, more obstructions in his way, and more

allurements to him to turn knave, than in any employment. . . .
[For] as getting money by all possible (fair) methods is his proper
business, and what he opens his shop for . . . 'tis not the easiest
thing in the world to distinguish between fair and foul, when 'tis
against himself" (*CET*, II, i, 33–34, 35). This candid recognition of
the traps of self-deception leads Defoe to a considerable degree of
tolerance. He cites the Golden Rule, "a perfect and unexceptiona-
ble rule" which "will hold for an unalterable law as long as there is
a tradesman left in the world." But, he goes on, "it may be said,
indeed, where is the man that acts thus? Where is the man whose
spotless integrity reaches it?" He offers those tradesmen who "if
they slip, are the first to reproach themselves with it; repent and
re-assume their upright conduct; the general tenor of whose lives is
to be honest and to do fair things. And this," he concludes, "is what
we may be allowed to call *an honest man;* for as to perfection, we are
not looking for it in life" (*CET*, II, i, 42).

More fundamental is the "paradox of trade and morality" that
Defoe recognizes as well as Mandeville: "the nation's prosperity is
built on the ruins of the nation's morals"; or, more cogently, "It
must be confessed, trade is almost universally founded upon crime."
By this Defoe means what Mandeville means: "What a poor nation
must we have been if we had been a sober, religious, temperate
nation? . . . The wealth of the country is raised by its wickedness,
and if it should be reformed it would be undone" (*CET*, II, ii, 105,
108, 106). Of luxury, Defoe could write "However it may be a vice
in morals, [it] may at the same time be a virtue in trade" (*Review*
III, 65–66). As Hans H. Anderson (from whose study I have drawn
several of these quotations) points out, Defoe does not try to shock
his readers as Mandeville does by insisting upon the irreducible
paradox; he tends to abstract issues and to exclude "ethical
considerations by the simple expedient of restricting his discussion
to what he called the 'Language of Trade.' " [4] But, although Defoe

---

[4] Hans H. Anderson, "The Paradox of Trade and Morality in Defoe," *Modern
Philology* 39 (1941), 35. The whole article is important (pp. 23–46).

does not take pleasure in the difficulties he creates for the moralist, he shows a keen awareness of the difficulties his characters encounter.

When Robinson Crusoe voices his satisfaction with his island, he finds it a place where the dangerous paradox is happily resolved.

> I was removed from all the wickedness of the world here. . . . I had nothing to covet; for I had all that I was now capable of enjoying. . . . There were no rivals; I had no competitor. . . . But all I could make use of was all that was valuable. . . . The most covetous griping miser in the world would have been cured of the vice of covetousness, if he had been in my case; for I possessed infinitely more than I knew what to do with (I, 142–43).

In short, Crusoe's island is the utopia of the Protestant Ethic (as Ian Watt puts it[5]) in a double sense. It is a place where Crusoe holds undistracted to his work and where his work is rewarded; but it is a place, too, where his tradesmanlike energy remains innocent, with no danger of inordinate desires leading to dishonesty. Only in the overambitious project of the *periagua* does Crusoe exceed the limits of utility, and the only consequences are the futility of wasted effort.

All of Defoe's other major characters yearn at one time or another for this freedom from the "necessity" embodied in temptation. The only other character who comes close to Crusoe's freedom is Colonel Jack in his management of slaves. Jack is concerned with the exploitation of his fellow men. Jack's master, the slaveowner, must exact obedience in order to realize the value of his property, but he would prefer to win voluntary service. Jack introduces a policy of mercy that wins the obligation of gratitude from the slave, Mouchat, and thus Jack reconciles trade (or here expediency) with morality and eliminates cruelty:

> if they were used with compassion, they would serve with affection as well as other servants . . . but never having been let taste what

[5] In "*Robinson Crusoe* as a Myth," *Essays in Criticism* I (1951) 95–119; as reprinted in *Eighteenth-Century English Literature: Modern Essays in Criticism*, ed. James L. Clifford, New York, 1959, p. 170.

mercy is, they know not how to act from a principle of love (X, 166–67).

Significantly, when Jack encounters a slave who will not learn this desirable lesson, he sells him off (X, 185); he can achieve his reconciliation only within the limits of the plantation, as Crusoe can his only in the isolation of his island kingdom. Both these scenes are, in effect, islands of ideal social order.

Later, when Jack is instructed in religious matters, he is made to see how God's mercy acts upon all men just as his own mercy has worked upon the slaves. The sense of mercy "seizes all the passions and all the affections, and works a sincere unfeigned abhorrence of the crime as a crime, as an offence against our Benefactor, as an act of baseness and ingratitude to Him who has given us our life . . . and who has conquered us by continuing to do us good when He has been provoked to destroy us" (X, 193). The "scholar" who instructs Jack proposes, somewhat in the spirit of Shaftesbury, that if men could see with full clarity the nature of both heaven and hell, "the first would have a stronger and more powerful effect to reform the world than the latter" (X, 194). This conception of a grateful man rejoicing in a merciful God is an ideal vision that Defoe would like to sustain. "But," as Jack remarks as he leaves home to wander in the world, "man is a short-sighted creature at best, and in nothing more than in that of fixing his own felicity, or, as we may say, choosing for himself" (XI, 107). We are back to Crusoe's "original sin" of leaving his father and the middle station of life, and in fact to all those expansive, restless efforts that are both the glory of the tradesman and the occasion for his temptations. The alternatives to this energy may be deadness of spirit or that serenity that at last confers "the leisure to repent." This leisure is given Defoe's characters intermittently in the course of their lives; only with age is it steadily achieved. Only after seventy-two years of a "life of infinite variety" does Crusoe fully "know the value of retirement, and the blessing of ending our days in peace."

Defoe's characters are all technicians, rational masters of their art, on one level, and creatures of impulse or obsession on another. When the young Robinson Crusoe hears his father's moving speech about the need to keep to the middle station of life, he is—as he tells us—"sincerely affected with this discourse . . . and I resolved not to think of going abroad any more, but to settle at home according to my father's wish." Then follows that verb that runs through Defoe's novels: "But alas! a few days wore it all off . . ." (I, 5). When a year later he goes to Hull, it is done "casually, and without any purpose of making an elopement that time"; yet on a sudden prompting he finds himself on board a ship bound for London. After escaping a dreadful storm that reveals all the horror and dangers of a life at sea, Crusoe is divided: he cannot face the shame of returning home, but he is still vividly aware of his career as a Jonah:

> An irresistible reluctance continued to going home; and, as I stayed awhile, the remembrance of the distress I had been in wore off; and as that abated, the little motion I had in my desires to a return wore off with it, till at last I quite laid aside the thoughts of it, and looked out for a voyage (I, 16).

This pattern is typical: the power of the impulse or obsession, the lack of clear decision; conflicts are settled in Crusoe or for him, not by him. Throughout his stay on the island, we see these fluctuations. Is the island a prison, or is it a deliverance from the sinful life he led in the world? Is the fate God has brought upon him an act of divine goodness, or is it fearfully inscrutable? All the trust he has achieved deserts him when he finds the footprint in the sand, and it is slowly regained. As he turns to Scripture and lights upon a telling verse, he finds comfort. "I thankfully laid down the book, and was no more sad," he tells us; and then adds, "at least, not on that occasion" (I, 175). There is always this note of reservation in Defoe's characters —as they prudently conceal some part of their fortune or story. It may be a note of mistrust, but, even more, it shows a sense, in the midst of joy or pleasure, that the mind of today need not be that of tomorrow, and perhaps cannot.

Moll Flanders, like Crusoe, is a creature of mixed and unstable motives. She goes to Bath, she tells us, "indeed in the view of taking what might offer; but I must do myself that justice as to protest I meant nothing but in an honest way, nor had any thoughts about me at first that looked the way which afterwards I suffered them to be guided" (VII, 106–7). It is sincere enough, but the moral twilight is clear, too. She lodges in the house of a woman "who, though she did not keep an ill house, yet had none of the best principles in her self" (VII, 107). When she has become the mistress of the gentleman she meets at Bath, she remarks that their living together was "the most undesigned thing in the world"; but in the next paragraph she adds: "It is true that from the first hour I began to converse with him I resolved to let him lie with me" (VII, 121). The surprise has come in finding that what she had been prepared to accept through economic necessity, she has encouraged through "inclination."

Earlier in America, when Moll discovers that she is married to her brother and the disclosure drives him to attempt suicide, she casts about:

> In this distress I did not know what to do, as his life was apparently declining, and I might perhaps have married again there, very much to my advantage, had it been my business to have stayed in the country; but my mind was restless too, I hankered after coming to England, and nothing would satisfy me without it (VII, 104).

Here, too, the motives are a wonderful mixture of concern, prudence, and impulse. What is most remarkable about Moll Flanders is her untroubled recognition of her motives, her readiness to set them forth with detachment, at least to the extent that she understands them. She recalls those Puritans who scrutinize their motives as if they were spectators beholding a mighty drama. When Moll robs a poor woman of the few goods that have survived a fire, she records:

> I say, I confess the inhumanity of the action moved me very much, and made me relent exceedingly, and tears stood in my eyes upon

that subject. But with all my sense of its being cruel and inhuman, I could never find it in my heart to make any restitution: the reflection wore off, and I quickly forgot the circumstances that attended it (VIII, 14).

Fielding was to make something beautifully ironic of this kind of mixture of motives. Defoe uses it differently; candor disarms the moral judgment that irony would require. The stress is more upon the energy of impulse than upon its evil. And the energy is such that it can scarcely be contained by a single motive or be channeled long in a consistent course.

The Question of Emotion in Defoe

by Benjamin Boyce

The Famous Mr. *Milton* wrote two Poems, *Paradise lost*, and *Paradise regain'd*, which tho' form'd in the same Mould, the Work of the same bright Genius, yet have met with a most differing Reception in the World; the first passes with a general Reputation for the greatest, best, and most sublime Work now in the *English* Tongue. . . . The other is call'd a Dull Thing, infinitely short of the former. . . . Mr. *Milton* was told this . . . and his Answer was this—Well, I see the Reason plainly . . . People have not the same Gust of Pleasure at the regaining Paradise, as they have Concern at the loss of it. . . .

(Defoe's *Review*, VIII, No. 63,
August 18, 1711)

Discussion of the work of Defoe has for many years centered on two main topics—his remarkable literary method, with its unprecedented plausibility and its exactitude, and the question of his personal morality. Opinion on both subjects has fallen into something of a pattern, with remarks to be made to Defoe's advantage and to his disadvantage on each. At the risk of pursuing novelty where none is to be found, I venture to suggest, first, that attention to Defoe's realistic method has caused critics to ignore one other source of his power—his representation of anxiety—and, second, that Defoe's success in this latter phase of his art was a result of his own problems of morality. I shall consider the former question first.

"The Question of Emotion in Defoe." From *Studies in Philology*, I (1953), 45–53. Reprinted by permission of The University of North Carolina Press.

I

Although Charles Lamb was one of the first critics to single out for praise Defoe's technique in realistic narrative, it was Leslie Stephen's long essay on Defoe's novels that established several now-familiar notions about his "most marvellous power . . . of giving verisimilitude to his fictions." The technique of the novels was to manufacture evidence for the truth of a story by calmly accumulating physical facts and economic circumstances. But this was done, said Stephen, at a high cost; there is, consequently, in the novels an almost total lack of "the passionate element"—almost no sense of sin, only slight attention to the "horrors" of Crusoe's situation, "no atom of sentiment" in the liaisons of Moll Flanders and Roxana, and a total lack of excitement in sex. Stephen's essay is vigorously written and it has had its effect. Virginia Woolf carried on the attack in her essay on *Robinson Crusoe* by requiring us to see that Defoe's "sense of reality" reduces all to "a plain earthenware pot." In the same tradition Queenie Leavis asserted that the period to which Defoe belonged was "hopelessly incurious where its feelings were concerned." Willa Cather in a sulky introduction to a new edition of *Roxana* complained that the book has no warmth, no feeling, and no "atmosphere." Ernest A. Baker explained this "lack of atmosphere" by referring to Defoe's concentration upon one character in each book and upon the problem of existence; Defoe's characters "have no time to indulge in emotion." Irving Howe lamented that Crusoe, though solitary, "never indulges in introspection." The point of view that Stephen presented [1] seems without exception to prevail.

[1] "Defoe's Novels," *Hours in a Library* (New York, 1894), I, 1–46. The other discussions alluded to in this paragraph are Virginia Woolf's "Robinson Crusoe" in *The Common Reader, Second Series* (London, 1932); Queenie D. Leavis's *Fiction and the Reading Public* (London, 1932), p. 105; Defoe's *The Fortunate Mistress . . . With an Introduction by Willa Cather* (New York, 1924); Ernest A. Baker's *History of the English Novel* (London), III (1929), 195–96; Irving Howe's "Robinson Crusoe: Epic of the Middle Class" in *Tomorrow*, VIII (1949), 51–54.

Undoubtedly the critics have grounds for their charges; but it would be well, in the first place, to see what the grounds of complaint are. All readers would agree that there are few passages, if any, in the novels of Defoe that suggest how rich the perceptions and emotions of a moment may be. Furthermore, by modern standards as well as Victorian, Defoe's books "play down" the thrills. Whether one's taste runs to *The Turn of the Screw* or to some of the more recent tales of mystery, it is obvious that the *Apparition of One Mrs. Veal* is a ghost-story totally without shudders. And whether one likes to read Henry Green's exquisitely tinted novels or merely the advertisements of the Great White Fleet's Caribbean cruises, it is true that in *Robinson Crusoe* one will find a tropical island which in the course of twenty-eight long years offers not one sunset or sunrise worth describing. William Dampier, the buccaneer-scientist whose abundant detail in *A New Voyage Round the World* made his book a valuable one for Defoe, supplemented his physical facts with such additional remarks as that seal-fur is handsome when wet, that coco-trees "make a very pleasant sight," and that the light-gray young flamingo eventually develops a "beautiful Shape" and "the Colour of new red Brick." [2] Crusoe, on the contrary, is not interested in the aesthetic aspects of his exotic surroundings, whether they be Morocco, Brazil, or the sea-ringed island. His parrot was presumably green, but we hardly know. To make matters worse, he seems to develop no feelings for his household pets. The cats merely became a nuisance, and one of the few comments we have on his dog, that fond friend of modern man, is that it "was now grown very old and crazy."

A more common disappointment is that though *Moll Flanders* and *Roxana* are stories of plentiful and prominent sexual adventure, they are without a single episode of romantic passion and, except for the brief and touching reunion of Moll and her Lancashire-husband Jemmy, without episodes of a sentimental sort. Seduction, marriage,

---

[2] *A New Voyage Round the World*, with an Introduction by Sir Albert Gray (London, 1937), pp. 69, 133, 57. I owe these references to Miss Joan E. Hartman.

bigamy, adultery, incest, the birth and loss of babies come and go without any full, climactic scenes. Every reader has been astonished by Defoe's way of presenting Moll's discovery that her husband, the father of two of her children and of one yet unborn, is her brother. But the absence of passion here is certainly proper. Moll asks anyone to judge of her feelings, and then quickly she faces the matter, as she did all matters, with a practical attitude. Here is a project; how best shall she manage it? Crusoe once cursed his "unlucky Head, that was always to let me know it was born to make my Body miserable"; it was always "fill'd with projects and designs" to get him off his island. But though he and Moll might curse their inventiveness, they were continually being saved by it. Moll's incestuous brother collapsed under the strain of their dilemma, but not Moll. Roxana, too, is a self-centered woman, whom Willa Cather found offensively unfeeling. Certainly Roxana *says* she was not moved by "the flames of desire," and Miss Cather is willing to believe her.

But both *Moll Flanders* and *Roxana* are seen to possess a certain kind of atmosphere, of emotional power, when we compare them with *Captain Singleton*, with *Colonel Jack*, and with *Memoirs of a Cavalier*. The difficulty in each of the latter romances is fundamentally, no doubt, one of characterization and point of view, questions we need not consider here except to say that in a technical sense *Memoirs of a Cavalier* is the most interesting. The creator of *Waverley* particularly admired it,[3] and Leslie Stephen, forgetting the effect of all but ten pages, carelessly dubbed it "a very amusing book." But it is the coldest of the three and for a reason that explains a basic weakness in *Captain Singleton* and in all but the boyhood scenes in *Colonel Jack*—the adventures evoke no feeling of alarm. We do not

[3] Sir Walter's judgment in these matters loses some of its authority when we discover that he or his friends the Ballantynes thought it a good idea, in their 1810 edition of the *Novels of Daniel DeFoe*, to delete the last six and a half paragraphs of *Robinson Crusoe* and attach to it, without warning, the much less interesting *Farther Adventures of Robinson Crusoe* as if they constituted a single work of art. One wonders how many nineteenth-century readers knew Defoe's work only in the Scott-Ballantyne version.

tremble for the hero's bodily or mental existence. What has made *Robinson Crusoe* a universally memorable book is not just the rather too frequently praised method of creating the impression of truth by tabulating articles owned and specifying the dimensions and processes of manufacture. Other books have that. Anyone who takes the trouble to compare William Dampier's description of how to catch the manatee or how the Indians of Colan build a bark-log raft[4] with Crusoe's account of how he added to the fortifications of his "castle" will see that Dampier comes closer than Defoe to meriting Stephen's phrase, "the amazing power of describing facts." Mark Schorer has made a helpful suggestion in saying that Defoe's "circumstantial realism" depends not on description but on proof of some kind.[5] One can go further. It is the emotional background, the often submerged but never quite forgotten anxiety, the recognition that any one stroke of the ax or slip of the judgment may end everything, that renders the detailing of processes and the totalling of resources so powerful. Defoe's methodical reporting and the emotional atmosphere of the book support and justify each other.

But the heart of the matter for our discussion of *Robinson Crusoe* is "the horrors of [Crusoe's] position," which were insufficiently developed to satisfy Leslie Stephen and which readers of Kafka and Koestler may also regard as strangely muted. But the horrors are unmistakably present. It is instructive to see how Crusoe reports on the emotional experience of crawling up alone on to an empty island. First we get a conventional narrator's account which will shock nobody and allow Crusoe-Defoe to proceed.

> I was now landed, and safe on Shore, and began to look up and thank God that my Life was sav'd in a Case wherein there was some Minutes before scarce any room to hope. I believe it is impossible to express to the Life what the Extasies and Transports of the Soul are, when it is so sav'd, as I may say, out of the very Grave; and I do not wonder now at that Custom, *viz.* That when a Malefactor who has

[4] *A New Voyage*, pp. 32, 102–4.

[5] "A Study in Defoe: Moral Vision and Structural Form," *Thought*, XXV (1950), 282.

the Halter about his Neck, is tyed up, and just going to be turn'd off, and has a Reprieve brought to him: I say, I do not wonder that they bring a Surgeon with it, to let him Blood that very Moment they tell him of it, that the Surprise may not drive the Animal Spirits from the Heart, and overwhelm him:

> *For sudden Joys, like Griefs, confound at first.*

I walk'd about on the Shore, lifting up my Hands, and my whole Being, as I may say, wrapt up in the Contemplation of my Deliverance, making a Thousand Gestures and Motions which I cannot describe, reflecting upon all my Comrades that were drown'd, and that there should not be one Soul sav'd but my self; for, as for them, I never saw them afterwards, or any Sign of them, except three of their Hats, one Cap, and two Shoes that were not Fellows.[6]

The final touch is much admired; the reference to the criminal saved from the noose is not. Defoe used the latter comparison again in the book for a similar experience. Crusoe was a criminal against God, Defoe thought, and the image is not inappropriate. But it is unexpected and not successful.

Thirty pages later, Crusoe tells us that it was only after he had recovered a little composure of mind on the island that he started keeping a journal. Had he begun sooner, he says, it would have been a shocking document.

> After I got to Shore and had escap'd drowning, instead of being thankful to God for my Deliverance, having first vomited with the great Quantity of salt Water which was gotten into my Stomach, and recovering my self a little, I ran about the Shore, wringing my Hands and beating my Head and Face, exclaiming at my Misery, and crying out, I was undone, undone, till tyr'd and faint I was forc'd to lye down on the Ground to repose, but durst not sleep for fear of being devour'd.

And for days, even in the process of unloading that huge stock of supplies from the ship, he would stop to search the horizon for a

[6] *Robinson Crusoe* (in *The Shakespeare Head Edition of the Novels and Selected Writings of Daniel Defoe* [Oxford]), I (1927), 51–52.

sail, then "sit down and weep like a child." The previous account, we now realize, had falsified the story in order to conceal agonies almost too painful to remember. When the journal is at last provided for us to see, the entry for the first day gives this famous island (the delight of every youthful reader) the name "the Island of Despair" and records only that the day was spent "in afflicting myself" and in terror. The truth is out. Augustan reticence about the horrors has not prevented Defoe's twice giving us plain hints of what "many dull things"—that is, what shocking, private, and indecorous things—would have gone into a stream-of-consciousness narrative. There is perhaps not "one statement of self-analysis" of the sort that Irving Howe and other modern intellectuals indulge in. But Crusoe tells us that on occasion his situation would burst upon him in anguish, "and my very Heart would die within me." [7] Nearly a hundred pages farther along, Crusoe tells of seeing another ship on his fatal rocks; but not one soul had survived.

> I cannot explain by any possible Energy of Words what a strange longing or hankering of Desires I felt in my Soul upon this Sight; breaking out sometimes thus: O that there had been but one or two; nay, or but one Soul sav'd out of this Ship, to have escap'd to me, that I might but have had one Companion, one Fellow-Creature to have spoken to me, and to have convers'd with! In all the Time of my solitary Life, I never felt so earnest, so strong a Desire after the Society of my Fellow-Creatures, or so deep a Regret at the want of it.
>
> There are some secret moving Springs in the Affections, which when they are set a going by some Object in view; or be it some Object, though not in view, yet rendred present to the Mind by the Power of Imagination, that Motion carries out the Soul by its Impetuosity to such violent eager embracings of the Object, that the Absence of it is insupportable.
>
> Such were these earnest Wishings, That but one Man had been sav'd! *O that it had been but One!* I believe I repeated the Words, *O that it had been but One!* a thousand Times; and the Desires were so mov'd by it, that when I spoke the Words, my Hands would clinch together, and my Fingers press the Palms of my Hands, that if I had

[7] *Ibid.,* p. 130.

had any soft Thing in my Hand, it would have crusht it involuntar-
ily; and my Teeth in my Head wou'd strike together, and set against
one another so strong, that for some time I cou'd not part them
again.[8]

The familiar episode of Crusoe's discovering the footprint, which
Robert Louis Stevenson called one of the great things in romance,
might also be re-examined by those who, like Stephen, regard
Robinson Crusoe as a book for boys, not men. To be sure, the terror
that develops in Crusoe after his initial surprise is primitive enough
for any boy to feel. Crusoe, having earlier been the mythic figure of
man born unwillingly into a strange and unfriendly universe (Defoe
calls attention to the mythic by having the island episode com-
mence on the anniversary of Crusoe's birth), at this point becomes
another symbolic figure, the man whose laboriously and painfully
achieved self-confidence in this difficult world is threatened by new
conditions, new enemies. Crusoe for two years is a haunted man.
His mind behaves strangely and so does his body, and his nights as
well as his days are fearful as he struggles with himself. After
"Weeks and Months" he succeeds in reviving his dead faith in God
and "was no more sad, at least, not on that Occasion." Ironic
reflection upon his reversed attitude toward the idea of society on
his island also cannot help the neurotic much. The extra fortifications he hurries into are described, and though the description is
really not clear, the sense of threat from "the Out-side of my outer
Wall" hits one forcibly. Eventually the savages are seen. Their
invasions come and depart, but the effect cannot equal that of the
previous invasion of fear. After the savages there is the final
invasion of white men. But the capture of Friday is the beginning of
the end of the emotional power of *Robinson Crusoe*. Fear of danger,
Crusoe says, is "ten thousand Times more terrifying than Danger it
self, when apparent to the Eyes," [9] and this book, in its central,
famous part, is loaded with fear. The critics have no doubt taken it

[8] *Ibid.,* pp. 217–18.
[9] *Ibid.,* p. 184.

for granted and forgotten it. Mrs. Woolf stubbornly talks only of Crusoe's stolidity of mind; indeed he is only too absurdly unlike the fear-haunted, island-confined sophisticates of her novels. But for him, as for her and for her characters, the terrors inescapably rise.

It is perhaps the unusual arrangement, in both *Moll Flanders* and *Roxana*, of presenting the sexual adventures in the first half of the book and developing emotional power in the second half that accounts for the bafflement of two such sensitive readers as Leslie Stephen and Willa Cather. Both critics speak, with signs of disappointment, of the lack of passion and even of erotic interest in the stories told by the two courtesans. Slums and houses of ill fame are made "deadly dull," Stephen thinks. *Roxana*, declares Miss Cather, is "as safe as sterilized gauze." But the copy of *Roxana* before me, taken from a college library, confutes their charges: Miss Cather's preface, with her scornful simile, is still in the volume but not the two leaves that would present Roxana's account of the debauching of Amy. It is true that Roxana explains that her "blood had no fire in it to kindle the flames of desire" and that she was kept in the trade so long only by avarice and vanity. But the evidence is against her; somewhat like Richardson's Pamela, Defoe's Roxana seems disinclined to see all in herself that we can see.

The interest provided by Defoe in the first half of *Roxana* includes much besides the erotic, but the real power of the book comes later, as Lamb noticed,[10] and it derives from the emotion of fear. There are skirmishes with this source of appeal early in the volume as soon as Roxana begins her life of adultery. And there is a favorite Defoe episode, fright aboard ship in a storm—sudden, crude, and easily forgotten. An evil jeweler pursues Roxana in Paris, but this story is a cloak-and-sword affair of slight emotional power. It is only when Roxana, after fifteen years abroad, begins to interest herself in finding and anonymously assisting her five abandoned children that real excitement develops. It begins casually with the discovery that

---

[10] See *The Letters of Charles and Mary Lamb*, ed. E. V. Lucas (London, 1912), II, 646–47.

one of Roxana's daughters has been a maid in her great London house. Defoe quickly builds up tensions, doing so, by the way, with the same high-handed indifference to chronology that Shakespeare allowed himself in telling a tale of intrigue. Roxana, wishing to retire with her wealth and avoid the strain of fast society, hides herself in the Minories and, masking as a Quaker, undertakes a new life of concealment and precarious happiness. But her interest in men and her past power over men quickly catch up with her. She cannot resist an encounter with an old lover, the Dutch merchant, and that means that her new life must be one of double deception. A kindly and honest man, the Dutchman proposes marriage, and she fraudulently and guiltily becomes his wife. But almost at the same time her servant-daughter becomes obsessed with a determination to find out who her benefactor is and who her mother is. Roxana's complicated deceptions are all threatened with exposure. The strain is the worse for her because she admires her Dutch husband. She also yearns (an improbability due to Defoe's attempting *decorum*) to hold the unhappy daughter in her arms; but of course Susan's recognition of her she fears more than anything else. The refusal of Roxana's friendly Quaker landlady to tell a literal lie multiplies the need of vigilant contriving and deception. Susan's *idée fixe* stirs up her emotions, and she drives her mother from one scheme of hiding to another, until, frightened, nervous, exhausted in body and mind, Roxana grows "sad, heavy, pensive and melancholy." She sleeps little and is close to hysteria; she dismisses her faithful maid Amy for offering to do away with Susan. Then she suspects that the murder has been done. She is a more agonizing spectacle than Crusoe in his haunted period because, unlike him, she is constantly and closely surrounded by people, and those who would befriend her are, unknown to themselves, those who terrify her. At this point Defoe apparently found his story too much for him and simply cut it off in a vague and inconclusive paragraph.

Defoe's novels lack romance and atmosphere of the kind made familiar by the nineteenth-century novelists who wrote of love. But they possess the romance of adventure, and they show Defoe to be an early experimenter with the atmosphere of anxiety. The "most forcibly urged emotion" in *Moll Flanders* is not affection nor spiritual despair nor avarice nor ambition; it is, as Mr. Schorer has said, a fear of Newgate.[11] Defoe's circumstantial realism is a technique which he developed early and which he could use in molding the older semi-literary patterns of travel book and introspective Puritan manual and criminal autobiography into new forms. Defoe's originality was of that sort. But where the books have emotional power—the island portion of *Robinson Crusoe*, the scenes in Colonel Jack's childhood, the latter parts of *Moll Flanders* and *Roxana*—they interest us by their evocation of some sort of fear. . . .

[11] "A Study in Defoe," p. 281.

Robinson Crusoe

by Ian Watt

We have until now been primarily concerned with the light which Defoe's first work of fiction sheds on the nature of the connections between economic and religious individualism and the rise of the novel; but since the primary reason for our interest in *Robinson Crusoe* is its literary greatness, the relation between that greatness and the way it reflects the deepest aspirations and dilemmas of individualism also requires brief consideration.

Robinson Crusoe falls most naturally into place, not with other novels, but with the great myths of Western civilisation, with *Faust*, *Don Juan* and *Don Quixote*. All these have as their basic plots, their enduring images, a single-minded pursuit by the protagonist of one of the characteristic desires of Western man. Each of their heroes embodies an *arete* and a *hubris*, an exceptional prowess and a vitiating excess, in spheres of action that are particularly important in our culture. Don Quixote, the impetuous generosity and the limiting blindness of chivalric idealism; Don Juan, pursuing and at the same time tormented by the idea of boundless experience of women; Faustus, the great knower, his curiosity always unsatisfied, and therefore damned. Crusoe, of course, seems to insist that he is not of their company; *they* are very exceptional people, whereas anyone would do what *he* did, in the circumstances. Yet he too has an exceptional prowess; he can manage quite on his own. And he has an excess: his inordinate egocentricity condemns him to isolation wherever he is.

"Robinson Crusoe." From *The Rise of the Novel: Studies in Defoe, Richardson and Fielding*, by Ian Watt, pp. 85–92. Originally published in 1957 by the University of California Press; reprinted by permission of The Regents of the University of California and Chatto and Windus Ltd., London.

The egocentricity, one might say, is forced on him, because he is cast away on an island. But it is also true that his character is throughout courting its fate and it merely happens that the island offers the fullest opportunity for him to realise three associated tendencies of modern civilisation—absolute economic, social and intellectual freedom for the individual.

It was Crusoe's realisation of intellectual freedom which made Rousseau propose the book as "the one book that teaches all that books can teach" for the education of Émile; he argued that "the surest way to raise oneself above prejudices, and order one's judgement on the real relationship between things, is to put oneself in the place of an isolated man, and to judge of everything as that man would judge of them according to their actual usefulness." [1]

On his island Crusoe also enjoys the absolute freedom from social restrictions for which Rousseau yearned—there are no family ties or civil authorities to interfere with his individual autonomy. Even when he is no longer alone his personal autarchy remains—indeed it is increased: the parrot cries out his master's name; unprompted Friday swears to be his slave for ever; Crusoe toys with the fancy that he is an absolute monarch; and one of his visitors even wonders if he is a god. [2]

Lastly, Crusoe's island gives him the complete *laissez-faire* which economic man needs to realise his aims. At home market conditions, taxation and problems of the labour supply make it impossible for the individual to control every aspect of production, distribution and exchange. The conclusion is obvious. Follow the call of the wide open places, discover an island that is desert only because it is barren of owners or competitors, and there build your personal Empire with the help of a Man Friday who needs no wages and makes it much easier to support the white man's burden.

Such is the positive and prophetic side of Defoe's story, the side which makes Crusoe an inspiration to economists and educators,

[1] *Émile, ou De l'éducation* (Paris, 1939), pp. 210, 214.
[2] *The Life and Strange Surprising Adventures of Robinson Crusoe*, ed. G. A. Aitken (London, 1902), pp. 226, 164, 300, 284.

and a symbol both for the displaced persons of urban capitalism, such as Rousseau, and for its more practical heroes, the empire builders. Crusoe realises all these ideal freedoms, and in doing so he is undoubtedly a distinctively modern culture-hero. Aristotle, for example, who thought that the man "who is unable to live in society, or who has no need because he is sufficient for himself, must be either a beast or a god," [3] would surely have found Crusoe a very strange hero. Perhaps with reason; for it is surely true that the ideal freedoms he achieves are both quite impracticable in the real world and in so far as they can be applied, disastrous for human happiness.

It may be objected that Robinson Crusoe's achievements are credible and wholly convincing. This is so, but only because in his narrative—perhaps as an unconscious victim of what Karl Mannheim has called the "Utopian mentality" which is dominated by its will to action and consequently "turns its back on everything which would shake its belief" [4] Defoe disregarded two important facts: the social nature of all human economies, and the actual psychological effects of solitude.

The basis for Robinson Crusoe's prosperity, of course, is the original stock of tools which he loots from the shipwreck; they comprise, we are told, "the biggest magazine of all kinds . . . that was ever laid up for one man." [5] So Defoe's hero is not really a primitive nor a proletarian but a capitalist. In the island he owns the freehold of a rich though unimproved estate. Its possession, combined with the stock from the ship, are the miracles which fortify the faith of the supporters of the new economic creed. But only that of the true believers: to the sceptic the classic idyll of free enterprise does not in fact sustain the view that anyone has ever attained comfort and security only by his own efforts. Crusoe is in fact the lucky heir to the labours of countless other individuals; his solitude is the measure, and the price of his luck, since it involves

[3] *Politics,* Bk. I, ch. 2.
[4] *Ideology and Utopia* (London, 1936), p. 36.
[5] *Life,* p. 60.

the fortunate decease of all the other potential stockholders; and the shipwreck, far from being a tragic peripety, is the *deus ex machina* which makes it possible for Defoe to present solitary labour, not as an alternative to a death sentence, but as a solution to the perplexities of economic and social reality.

The psychological objection to *Robinson Crusoe* as a pattern of action is also obvious. Just as society has made every individual what he is, so the prolonged lack of society actually tends to make the individual relapse into a straightened primitivism of thought and feeling. In Defoe's sources for *Robinson Crusoe* what actually happened to the castaways was at best uninspiring. At worst, harassed by fear and dogged by ecological degradation, they sank more and more to the level of animals, lost the use of speech, went mad, or died of inanition. One book which Defoe had almost certainly read, *The Voyages and Travels of J. Albert de Mandelslo*, tells of two such cases; of a Frenchman who, after only two years of solitude on Mauritius, tore his clothing to pieces in a fit of madness brought on by a diet of raw tortoise; and of a Dutch seaman on St. Helena who disinterred the body of a buried comrade and set out to sea in the coffin.[6]

These realities of absolute solitude were in keeping with the traditional view of its effects, as expressed by Dr. Johnson: the "solitary mortal," he averred, was "certainly luxurious, probably superstitious, and possibly mad: the mind stagnates for want of employment; grows morbid, and is extinguished like a candle in foul air." [7]

In the story just the opposite happens: Crusoe turns his forsaken estate into a triumph. Defoe departs from psychological probability in order to redeem his picture of man's inexorable solitariness, and it is for this reason that he appeals very strongly to all who feel isolated—and who at times does not? An inner voice continually suggests to us that the human isolation which individualism has

---

[6] See A. W. Secord, *Studies in the Narrative Method of Defoe* (Urbana, 1924), pp. 28–29.

[7] *Thraliana*, ed. K. Balderston (Oxford, 1951), I, 180.

fostered is painful and tends ultimately to a life of apathetic animality and mental derangement; Defoe answers confidently that it can be made the arduous prelude to the fuller realisation of every individual's potentialities; and the solitary readers of two centuries of individualism cannot but applaud so convincing an example of making a virtue out of a necessity, so cheering a colouring to that universal image of individualist experience, solitude.

That it is universal—the word that is always to be found inscribed on the other side of the coin of individualism—can hardly be doubted. We have already seen how, although Defoe himself was an optimistic spokesman of the new economic and social order, the unreflecting veracity of his vision as a novelist led him to report many of the less inspiring phenomena associated with economic individualism which tended to isolate man from his family and his country. Modern sociologists have attributed very similar consequences to the other two major trends which are reflected in *Robinson Crusoe*. Max Weber, for example, has shown how the religious individualism of Calvin created among its adherents a historically unprecedented "inner isolation";[8] while Émile Durkheim derived from the division of labour and its associated changes many of the endless conflicts and complexities of the norms of modern society, the *anomie*[9] which sets the individual on his own and, incidentally, provides the novelists with a rich mine of individual and social problems when he portrays the life of his time.

Defoe himself seems to have been much more aware of the larger representativeness of his epic of solitude than is commonly assumed. Not wholly aware, since, as we have seen, he departed from its actual economic and psychological effects to make his hero's struggles more cheering than they might otherwise have been; nevertheless Crusoe's most eloquent utterances are concerned with solitude as the universal state of man.

The *Serious Reflections of Robinson Crusoe* (1720) are actually a

[8] *Protestant Ethic*, p. 108.
[9] *De la division du travail social*, Bk. II, chs. 1 and 3.

miscellaneous compilation of religious, moral and thaumaturgic material, and cannot, as a whole, be taken seriously as a part of the story: the volume was primarily put together to cash in on the great success of the first part of the trilogy, *The Life and Strange Surprising Adventures*, and the smaller one of the *Further Adventures*. There are, however, in the prefaces, and the first essay, "On Solitude," a number of valuable clues as to what, on second thoughts at least, Defoe saw as the meaning of his hero's experiences.

In "Robinson Crusoe's Preface" he suggests that the story "though allegorical, is also historical": it is based on the life of "a man alive, and well known too, the actions of whose life are the just subject of these volumes, and to whom all or most part of the story most directly alludes"; and Defoe hints that he is himself the "original" of which Robinson Crusoe is the "emblem"; that it is his own life which he is portraying allegorically.

Many critics have denied, and even derided the claim. *Robinson Crusoe* had apparently been attacked as fictitious, and it is argued that Defoe was merely using the allegorical argument very largely to controvert this criticism, and also to alleviate the popular Puritan aversion to fiction which he largely shared. Still, the claim to some autobiographical relevance cannot be wholly rejected: *Robinson Crusoe* is the only book for which he made the claim; and it fits in very well with much of what we know of Defoe's outlook and aspirations.

Defoe was himself an isolated and solitary figure in his time; witness the summary of his own life which he wrote in the preface to a 1706 pamphlet, *A Reply to a Pamphlet, Entitled "The Lord Haversham's Vindication of His Speech . . ."* where he complains:

> how I stand alone in the world, abandoned by those very people that own I have done them service; . . . how, with . . . no helps but my own industry, I have forced misfortune, and reduced them, exclusive of composition, from seventeen to less than five thousand pounds; how, in gaols, in retreats, in all manner of extremities, I have supported myself without the assistance of friends or relations.

"Forcing his way with undiscouraged diligence" is surely the heroism which Crusoe shares with his creator: and in "Robinson Crusoe's Preface" it is this quality which he mentions as the inspiring theme of his book: "Here is invincible patience recommended under the worst of misery, indefatigable application and undaunted resolution under the greatest and most discouraging circumstances."

Having asserted an autobiographical meaning for his story, Defoe goes on to consider the problem of solitude. His discussion is an interesting illustration of Weber's view of the effects of Calvinism. Most of the argument is concerned with the Puritan insistence on the need for the individual to overcome the world in his own soul, to achieve a spiritual solitude without recourse to monasticism. "The business is to get a retired soul," he says, and goes on: "All the parts of a complete solitude are to be as effectually enjoyed, if we please, and sufficient grace assisting, even in the most populous cities, among the hurries of conversation and gallantry of a court, or the noise and business of a camp, as in the deserts of Arabia and Lybia, or in the desolate life of an uninhabited island."

This note, however, occasionally relapses into a more general statement of solitude as an enduring psychological fact: "All reflection is carried home, and our dear self is, in one respect, the end of living. Hence man may be properly said to be alone in the midst of crowds and the hurry of men and business. All the reflections which he makes are to himself; all that is pleasant he embraces for himself; all that is irksome and grievous is tasted but by his own palate." [10] Here the Puritan insistence on possessing one's soul intact from a sinful world is couched in terms which suggest a more absolute, secular and personal alienation from society. Later this echo of the redefined aloneness of Descartes's *solus ipse* modulates into an anguished sense of personal loneliness whose overpowering reality moves Defoe to his most urgent and moving eloquence:

[10] G. A. Aitken, ed., *Serious Reflections of Robinson Crusoe* (London, 1902), pp. 7, 15, 2, 2–3.

What are the sorrows of other men to us, and what their joy? Something we may be touched indeed with by the power of sympathy, and a secret turn of the affections; but all the solid reflection is directed to ourselves. Our meditations are all solitude in perfection; our passions are all exercised in retirement; we love, we hate, we covet, we enjoy, all in privacy and solitude. All that we communicate of those things to any other is but for their assistance in the pursuit of our desires; the end is at home; the enjoyment, the contemplation, is all solitude and retirement; it is for ourselves we enjoy, and for ourselves we suffer.

"We covet, we enjoy, all in privacy and solitude": what really occupies man is something that makes him solitary wherever he is, and too aware of the interested nature of any relationship with other human beings to find any consolation there. "All that we communicate . . . to any other is but for their assistance in the pursuit of our desires": a rationally conceived self-interest makes a mockery of speech; and the scene of Crusoe's silent life is not least a Utopia because its functional silence, broken only by an occasional "Poor Robinson Crusoe" from the parrot, does not impose upon man's ontological egocentricity the need to assume a false façade of social intercourse, or to indulge in the mockery of communication with his fellows.

Robinson Crusoe, then, presents a monitory image of the ultimate consequences of absolute individualism. But this tendency, like all extreme tendencies, soon provoked a reaction. As soon as man's aloneness was forced on the attention of mankind, the close and complex nature of the individual's dependence on society, which had been taken for granted until it was challenged by individualism, began to receive much more detailed analysis. Man's essentially social nature, for instance, became one of the main topics of the eighteenth-century philsophers; and the greatest of them, David Hume, wrote in the *Treatise of Human Nature* (1739) a passage which might almost have been a refutation of *Robinson Crusoe*:

> We can form no wish which has not a reference to society. . . . Let all the powers and elements of nature conspire to serve and obey one

man; let the sun rise and set at his command; the sea and rivers roll
as he pleases, and the earth still furnish spontaneously whatever may
be useful or agreeable to him; he will still be miserable, till you give
him one person at least with whom he may share his happiness, and
whose esteem and friendship he may enjoy.[11]

Just as the modern study of society only began once individualism had focussed attention on man's apparent disjunctions from his
fellows, so the novel could only begin its study of personal
relationships once *Robinson Crusoe* had revealed a solitude that cried
aloud for them. Defoe's story is perhaps not a novel in the usual
sense since it deals so little with personal relations. But it is
appropriate that the tradition of the novel should begin with a work
that annihilated the relationships of the traditional social order,
and thus drew attention to the opportunity and the need of building
up a network of personal relationships on a new and conscious
pattern; the terms of the problem of the novel and of modern
thought alike were established when the old order of moral and
social relationships was shipwrecked, with Robinson Crusoe, by the
rising tide of individualism.

[11] Bk. II, pt. 2, sect. v.

Robinson Crusoe's Original Sin

by Maximillian E. Novak

Modern critics have applied the theories of Marx, Max Weber, and R. H. Tawney to Crusoe's island so often that it has become commonplace to suggest that the key to Defoe lies in an understanding of capitalism and economic individualism. That there is an economic problem in *Robinson Crusoe* is beyond question. The opening pages of the novel present a clear conflict between the hero and his father on the issue of Crusoe's future profession and social status. But the exact nature of this problem has been obscured by the neglect of two important points: Defoe's economic ideas and Crusoe's fictional character. Throughout his narrative Crusoe is aware of a terrible "original sin" against his father and God—a sin which he regards as the direct cause of all his suffering. I suggest that Crusoe's sin is his refusal to follow the "calling" chosen for him by his father, and that the rationale for this action may be found in Crusoe's personal characteristics: his lack of economic prudence, his inability to follow a steady profession, his indifference to a calm bourgeois life, and his love of travel.

Such a view seems a complete contradiction of the Crusoe who has been made the hero of numerous economic utopias, where he is invariably cast in the role of economic man. Before examining Crusoe's character in detail, we must consider the reasons for this

"Robinson Crusoe's Original Sin." From *The Economics and the Fiction of Daniel Defoe*, by M. E. Novak, University of California Press Publications in English Studies, Vol. 24 (1962), pp. 32–48. Originally published in 1962 by the University of California Press; reprinted by permission of The Regents of the University of California.

contradiction and examine Defoe's approach to man as an economic animal. Adam Smith, who is often credited with the invention of economic man, constructed his theories on the fundamental assumptions of human selfishness and self-interest. These qualities, Smith believed, belonged to all classes of men, but more particularly to merchants and manufacturers who, with their "superior knowledge of their own interest," have often tricked the nation into believing that the interest of the middle class was the same as that of the public. Accompanying economic man's realization of his own interest is his dissatisfaction with his present lot. Thus arises, wrote Smith, "the desire of bettering our condition, a desire which, though generally calm and dispassionate, comes with us from the womb, and never leaves us till we go into the grave." [1] Never satisfied, economic man denies himself present enjoyment, saves and invests his money, and, if he has not become too avaricious, may live to enjoy future benefits.

His only virtue is prudence, which Smith believed was the dominant trait in all men. But although Veblen regarded prudence as the sole "human" characteristic of economic man, it is hardly a satisfactory substitute for all the Christian virtues. A world based on this abstraction would be a return to the jungle. Smith justified the existence of economic man, however, by arguing an "unseen hand," which would turn all private selfishness into public good. "Every individual," he wrote, "is continually exerting himself to find out the most advantageous employment for whatever capital he can command. It is his own advantage, indeed, and not that of society, which he has in view. . . . But the study of his own advantage naturally, or rather necessarily, leads him to prefer that employment which is most advantageous to the society." [2] This was a distinctly eighteenth-century solution in which the theme was "partial evil, universal good," yet it was generally accepted in the

[1] *The Wealth of Nations* (Everyman Library ed.; London, 1954), I, 398, 305.
[2] *Ibid.*, I, 398.

first half of the next century as a sanctification of the selfish activity
of the entrepreneur.

As an opponent of free trade and *laissez faire,* Defoe had very
different attitudes toward economic man. Smith had not invented
economic man, but had merely inherited him from the mercantil-
ists. He was an abstraction of the merchant, a superman whose
unholy prophets were Machiavelli and Hobbes. To Machiavelli's
view of man as an evil and acquisitive animal, Hobbes added the
concept of a being whose "natural" elements were equality,
self-interest, appetite, avarice, and a general desire for activity.
Although Hobbes aroused a storm of disapprobation in the realms
of religion and philosophy, he was a major influence in the
economic attitudes of Petty, Child, and Davenant.[3] And Defoe, who
proclaimed that Hobbes had an "exalted spirit in Philosophy" in
spite of his unfortunate religious opinions, clearly accepted an
economic psychology not very different from that of the iconoclast
of Malmesbury.[4] As Heckscher has remarked, the mercantilist
economists were amoral in both their aims and means and
"indifferent towards mankind, both in its capacity as a reasoning
animal, and also in its attitude towards the eternal."[5] They
postulated a natural man, free from religion and positive laws, with
a drive to better his condition, not so much for the purpose of
self-improvement, like Smith's creation, as from an innate restlessness and a desire for power.

To what extent did Defoe apply these concepts to his economic
writings? Like Hobbes, he accepted the concept of natural equality,
although he believed that men of superior talents usually found
their way into the middle classes or the aristocracy. He also
followed Hobbes in founding his economics on a belief in human
selfishness and the conviction that most men follow their own
interests. In *Jure Divino,* he stated as an axiom:

[3] For the influence of Hobbes on these economists, see William Petty, *Economic
Writings,* ed. Charles Hull (Cambridge, Eng., 1899), I, lxi–lxiii; Josiah Child, *A
Discourse about Trade* (London, 1690), p. 125; and Charles Davenant, *Discourses on the
Public Revenues, and on Trade* (London, 1698), p. 263.

[4] *The Storm* (London, 1704), p. 4.

[5] Eli Heckscher, *Mercantilism,* trans. Mandel Shapiro (London, 1935), II, 285.

> Self-Love's the Ground of all the things we do,
> Which they that talk on't least do most pursue,

adding the footnote that "Self-interest is such a prevailing bond, especially when Reason concurs, that it never fails to open Men's Eyes to their own Advantages, when they are brought to extremities." [6] And in arguing against the Whig attempt to withdraw credit from the government in 1712, he affirmed his conviction that men would always place economic considerations above political allegiance, for to "pretend . . . that Parties shall Govern Mankind against their Gain, is to Philosophize wisely upon what *may be,* and what would be Politick to bring to pass; but what no Man can say was ever put into practise to any Perfection." [7] Indeed he referred to self-interest as "that immortal . . . Bond of Trade," for without it all business dealings would be uncertain.[8]

Defoe was fond of quoting Lord Rochester's line, "In my dear self I centre everything," and like that poet, he regarded self-interest as instinctual. But he also recognized that "Men do not always pursue their own Interest," and he felt that the task of the economic propagandist was to convince his readers that a particular act or law was intended for their personal benefit.[9] " 'Tis only opening the Eyes of the Men in Trade," he wrote, "that can bring these things to pass; and how that can be done when their own Interest will not do it, I confess is hard to imagine." [10]

But while accepting self-interest as the basis of human action, Defoe did not believe that it would lead to the good of society. Basing his arguments on the "Nature of Man; which forbids him being satisfied with anything less *than all he can get,*" he urged the government to pass a variety of laws which would control the freedom of economic man.[11] In proposing a bill to prevent English

---

[6] (London, 1706), Bk. IV, p. 8.
[7] *An Essay upon Loans* (London, 1710), p. 15.
[8] *A Plan of the English Commerce* (Shakespeare Head ed.), p. 271.
[9] *Review,* V, 599a.
[10] *Ibid.,* III, 23a.
[11] William Lee, *Daniel Defoe: His Life and Recently Discovered Writings* (London, 1869), III, 211.

commerce from having any contact with areas infected by plague in Marseilles, he commented sadly on the necessity of governmental action against the enterprising but dangerous merchant. "Men will risk their Lives," he complained, "and the Lives of a whole City, nay a whole Nation, for their present Profit; by not putting any Dangers . . . in the Scale with their present Advantages. Give them the Gain they have in View, and the present Advances of their Fortunes and Estates; and as for the Consequences, leave it to them, and leave them to their Fate." [12] Not that he found it at all incredible that a merchant should endanger the entire nation "for the wretched Gain of a private Man." He argued that such greed should be expected, controlled, and punished with the utmost severity by the state.

If Defoe used economic man in his fiction, his view of him would of necessity be ambiguous. He admired the merchant, but not the capitalist or even the tradesman who made excessive profits. In 1719, the year of the publication of *Robinson Crusoe*, Defoe launched an attack upon stockjobbing, the South Sea Company, and the East India Company. And in the same year he turned his mind away from the home trade to urge colonization of the area around the Orinoco, where Raleigh had explored and Crusoe was to be cast away. When he created the character of Crusoe, Defoe certainly had more empathy with the concept of the colonist than with that of the capitalist. But the dreams of Raleigh were more the concern of the seventeenth century, when Cromwell used the *History of the World* as bed-time reading, than of the century that was preparing to experience the boom-and-bust cycle of the South Sea Bubble. We might expect, therefore, that economic primitivism, not economic progress, would be the theme of a fictional work by Defoe. Economic man might have been the villain of the piece; he could never have been the hero.

An artistic problem is also involved. Economic man is too single-minded to be anything more than a minor character,

[12] *Ibid.,* II, 408.

perhaps an embodiment of avarice, in a work of fiction. Defoe's attitude toward self-love must be kept in mind as we try to understand the motivation of his characters, but we must also remember his acknowledgment that human beings were often moved by considerations both entirely noneconomic and opposed to self-interest. In turning to a thorough analysis of Crusoe's thoughts and actions, we discover a complex and fully developed personality whose main interests have little to do with the pursuit of wealth.

Crusoe gives an excellent sketch of his character toward the end of the *Farther Adventures*. Abandoned by his mutinous crew at Bengal, he has entered into partnership with a hard-working merchant whose plodding, diligent character Crusoe finds in direct contrast to his own:

> But my Fellow Traveller and I, had different Notions; I do not name this, to insist upon my own, for I acknowledge his were the most just and the most suited to the end of a Merchant's Life; who, when he is abroad upon Adventures, 'tis his Wisdom to stick to that as the best Thing for him, which he is like to get the most Money by: My new Friend kept himself to the Nature of the Thing, and would have been content to have gone like a Carrier's Horse, always to the same Inn, backward and Forward, provided he could, as he call'd it, *find his Account in it;* on the other Hand, mine was the Notion of a mad rambling Boy, that never cares to see a Thing twice over.[13]

The Crusoe who describes himself as a "mad rambling Boy" may have been ignored by recent critics, but this is not his entire character. When his partner reproaches him for his lack of ambition and his avarice, Crusoe retorts, "Once I conquer my backwardness, and embark heartily; as old as I am, I shall harrass you up and down the World, till I tire you; for I shall pursue it so eagerly, I shall never let you lye still" (III, 112).

Crusoe's conversion to the "Principles of Merchandizing" is, as usual, short-lived, but the character he gives himself in this section is certainly the best glimmer of self-knowledge presented to the

---

[13] *Robinson Crusoe* (Shakespeare Head ed.), III, 111. (Subsequent citations of Defoe's novels enclosed within parentheses in my text will refer to this edition.)

reader. Interpretations of Crusoe as the average Englishman, as everyman, as economic man, or as a self-portrait of Defoe, have tended to obscure his real personality. For Crusoe is a prototype of Shaw's Bluntschli—the hero raised as a tradesman but with a romantic temperament. Whenever he finds himself compelled to work, he is talented enough to succeed, but, as Crusoe reminds us, he was "possest with a wandring Spirit" (III, 80) which would never let him remain in one spot for very long. This, of course, is why his punishment is so appropriate. To be abandoned on an island for twenty-eight years was even more of a torture for the restless Crusoe than it would be for most men.

Although an awareness of Crusoe's restlessness and desire for travel provides an insight into his reason for leaving his father's house, it does not explain why he regarded this action as his "original sin." This problem was as puzzling to a contemporary critic like Charles Gildon as it has been to the moderns. Gildon suggested that Defoe was trying to insult the English navy; Paul Dottin appealed to the power of the father in Puritan homes; and Ian Watt has argued that Crusoe's sin was "really the dynamic tendency of capitalism itself" and part of his desire to improve his economic status.[14] None of these explanations is entirely satisfactory. The opening remarks in the debate between Crusoe and his father involve a problem of economic or social class, but there is little indication that Crusoe is trying to improve his economic status. If that were his intention, Crusoe would have to be foolish indeed if the strong arguments of his father did not convince him that the steady road of middle-class life was the best way to wealth and happiness.

Crusoe's father attempts to win his son over by appealing to his self-interest. He tells Crusoe that the life of a man firmly rooted in the middle class is happy because it is safe and comfortable, whereas the life of an adventurer usually results in poverty, or, if successful, in the discontent and the luxury of the upper classes:

[14] Cf. Charles Gildon, *The Life and Strange Surprising Adventures of Mr. D—— De F——*, in *Robinson Crusoe Examin'd and Criticis'd*, ed. Paul Dottin (London, 1923), p. 84; and Ian Watt, *The Rise of the Novel* (London, 1957), p. 65.

> He told me . . . that these things were all either too far above me, or
> too far below me; that mine was the middle State, or what might be
> called the upper Station of *Low Life*, which he had found by long
> Experience was the best State in the World, the most suited to
> human Happiness, not exposed to the Miseries and Hardships, the
> Labour and Sufferings of the mechanick Part of Mankind, and not
> embarrass'd with the Pride, Luxury, Ambition and Envy of the
> upper Part of Mankind. . . .
>
>   He bid me observe . . . that the middle Station had the fewest
> Disasters, and was not expos'd to so many Vicissitudes as the higher
> or lower Part of Mankind; . . . not embarrass'd with the Labours of
> the Hands or of the Head, not sold to the Life of Slavery for daily
> Bread, or harrast with perplex'd Circumstances, which rob the soul
> of Peace and the Body of Rest. . . . (I, 2)

Of course this is not only good economic advice; it is also the
counsel of age to youth. But it is not the kind of appeal that will
move Crusoe, who is indifferent to comfort and whose head is filled
with thoughts of travel and adventure.

Eventually Crusoe comes to regard his life as a "Memento" of
God's revenge upon a man who leaves his station, disobeys his
parents, and abandons his calling. But is Crusoe's desire to go to sea
so unreasonable? And how practical were his father's plans to
establish him as a lawyer or a tradesman? Even Gildon found this
puzzling, for we learn nothing more about Crusoe's prospects than
his father's guarantee that he would be comfortably provided for if
he remained in the "middle station" of life.[15] Because the way to
wealth in the seventeenth century was either through trade or
through the law, these are important considerations in determining
Crusoe's motives in refusing to accept the position in life chosen for
him by his father. There seems little doubt that by applying himself
to either of these professions Crusoe would have become wealthy.[16]
Crusoe vaguely suggests that he wanted to raise his fortune, but as

---

[15] *Op. cit.*, p. 83.

[16] For information on the best careers open to Crusoe see H. R. Trevor-Roper,
The Gentry, 1540–1640 (London, 1953), pp. 13–27; and John H. Plumb, *Sir Robert
Walpole* (London, 1956), pp. 18–28.

his father clearly points out, the sea was only for those of great wealth or of "desperate Fortunes" (I, 2). The dreams of riches from sea adventures had faded with Raleigh in the Tower. Thus the suggestion that Crusoe's main interest was to improve his condition in life seems to confuse the restlessness of the capitalist with the restlessness of the wanderer.[17] Dottin was at least partially correct in arguing that "Defoe's intention was to represent a rash and inconsiderate boy, unable to resist the strong impulse that urged him to a seafaring life." [18]

But Dottin failed to realize that Crusoe's behavior involved a sin against a specific religious-economic doctrine. Some similar historical examples will be illuminating here. Richard Norwood, the first surveyor of Bermuda, who ran away from home to go to sea, was haunted with remorse over his disobedience to his parents and his failure to follow the calling they selected for him. He became angry when a minister told him that the evils that had befallen him at sea were the result of his failure to follow his calling, but in his meditations he upbraided himself for having "forsaken the calling wherein . . . [his] parents had placed . . . [him] and betaken . . . [himself] to another course of life without any due calling or encouragement from God or men." [19] And Cotton Mather, in a tract on the execution of twenty-six pirates, moralizes chiefly on their disobedience to their parents in not following the calling chosen for them. Among those pirates who repented was John Browne, who testified to the folly of rebelling against one's parents. "Stay in your Place & Station Contentedly," he advised the reader.[20]

[17] The economist Thomas Ashton observed that *Robinson Crusoe* was the "epic of the ordinary man" during the eighteenth century because it inspired both the urge to go to sea which made England a great naval power and the interest in inventions which produced the Industrial Revolution. See Ashton, *An Economic History of England: The 18th Century* (London, 1955), p. 105.

[18] *Op. cit.,* p. 152.

[19] *The Journal of Richard Norwood*, ed. Wesley Craven and Walter Hayward (New York, 1945), pp. 16–33.

[20] *Useful Remarks* (New-London, 1723), pp. 23, 31–33.

Crusoe's concern over disobeying his father's advice follows the same pattern. Boarding a ship for London, he is confronted by two storms, and, although a passenger, is forced to labor at the pumps where he faints from fright. He narrates his salvation as a kind of miracle and persists in viewing these tempests as punishment for his sin and as the fulfillment of his father's prediction that God would not bless him and that he would have leisure to repent when it was too late. Although Crusoe's father was merely prophesying his son's future, his words have the operative power of a curse; Crusoe never forgets them: "I began now seriously to reflect upon what I had done, and how justly I was overtaken by the Judgment of Heaven for my wicked leaving my Father's House, and abandoning my Duty," he remarks after his first misadventure; "all the good Counsel of my Parents, my Father's Tears and my Mother's Entreaties came now fresh into my Mind; and my Conscience . . . reproach'd me with the Contempt of Advice, and the Breach of Duty to God and my Father" (I, 7). Crusoe's reaction might seem extreme to the modern reader, but it reveals the same connection between the will of God and the will of the parent in the choice of an occupation that we have already seen in Norwood's and Mather's reflections on this subject.

From these examples it might be expected that the doctrine of the calling was always used to invoke obedience, but Weber and Tawney have argued that Luther's concept of the *Beruf* eventually became a formative influence in the development of economic individualism and capitalism. As developed by Luther, this doctrine was associated with a rigidly stratified society and with the sanctification of work. Both of these ideas appear in a poem by the sixteenth-century poet Robert Crowley, who warned the merchant that he would be "damned eternally" if he attempted to raise himself or his son to a higher station in life:

> For in the worlde ther can not be
> More greate abhomination,

To thy Lord God, then is in the
Forsakeyng thy vocation.[21]

Long before 1719, when *Robinson Crusoe* was first published,
Protestant sects had changed Luther's doctrine into a proof of
salvation by works or, more specifically, by work. Because he
believed that salvation and election depended only upon God's
grace, the Protestant appealed to the evidence of worldly success as
visible proof of God's favor. "The Calling," wrote Tawney, "is not a
condition in which the individual is born, but a strenuous and
exacting enterprise to be undertaken indeed, under the guidance of
Providence, but to be chosen by each man for himself, with a deep
sense of his solemn responsibilities." [22] Although the skeleton of
Luther's idea remained, the central concept of a stratified society,
whose functions had been governed by rules of the Church,
disappeared before the conviction that each man had the right to
attain an economic status commensurate with his abilities and with
God's favor.

To apply the theories of economic individualism to *Robinson
Crusoe* might seem appropriate in view of Defoe's pride in the rise of
the middle class and his praise of intermarriage between merchant
families and the nobility.[23] But everything in *Robinson Crusoe* related
to the calling constitutes an attack upon economic individualism.
Interestingly enough, H. M. Robertson in his refutation of some of
Tawney's theories selected Defoe as one of the few economic
thinkers who attacked those tradesmen who sought more than a
moderate degree of wealth and who advanced the conservative
ideal of the calling as "an invitation to live the orderly and settled
life ordained by God, and to perform all duties pertaining to it." [24]
And in 1720, amid the frenzied buying and selling of South Sea

[21] *Select Works* (London, 1872), p. 90.
[22] R. H. Tawney, *Religion and the Rise of Capitalism* (London, 1926), p. 241. See
also Max Weber, *The Protestant Ethic and the Spirit of Capitalism*, trans. Talcott
Parsons (New York, 1950), pp. 52–56, 80–88.
[23] See, for example, *What If the Swedes Should Come* (London, 1717), p. 19.
[24] *Aspects of the Rise of Economic Individualism* (Cambridge, Eng., 1933), p. 11.

stock, Defoe reminded the merchant of the limits of his station. "What have Merchants to do to turn Gamesters?" he asked. "What have Linnen and Woollen Men to do with Box and Dice? Every man to his Business! Let them mind their Calling and leave the Bites and Cullies to the Place of the Bites and Cullies. . . ." [25]

Although Defoe's economic ideas were unquestionably conservative, I do not wish to suggest that they were anachronistic. In his *Complete English Tradesman* Defoe argued that a man might change his calling, and made no equation of God's will with parental choice of occupation. His advice to the tradesman has the same implications as the counsel of Crusoe's father: "Let the wise and wary Tradesman take the Hint, keep within the Bounds where Providence has placed him, be content to rise gradually and gently, . . . and as he is sufficiently rich . . . go softly on, least he comes not softly down." [26] In *Serious Reflections of Robison Crusoe* the hero criticizes parents who choose callings for their children which are unsuited to their natural abilities, but this is not meant as a reproach to his own parents, who would have been content with any steady profession which their son might have selected.[27] In opposition to his father's advice, Crusoe can offer only a desire to travel.

Before making any final judgment of Defoe's attitude, let us turn to the narrative itself and Crusoe's interpretation of events. Crusoe leaves his father's home against his father's advice and with the awareness of God's revenge against disobedience, a revenge revealed in the disappearance of his two brothers who also ran away and abandoned their callings. But instead of returning to York, he persists in following "the Dictates of . . . [his] Fancy rather than

[25] Lee, *op. cit.*, II, 203. See also Defoe's essay on discontent, "The Original of Original Sin," as the cause of the wild financial speculation in 1720. *The Commentator*, no. 40 (May 20, 1720).

[26] (London, 1727), II, 96.

[27] *Romances and Narratives by Daniel Defoe*, ed. George Aitken (London, 1895), III, 62–64. (This will be cited subsequently as Dent ed.) Crusoe's parents send him money when they discover that he is going to Africa for the purpose of trade. See *Robinson Crusoe* (Shakespeare Head ed.), I, 18.

. . . [his] Reason" (I, 45). Does Crusoe's disobedience have any
effect on the events of the story? Crusoe himself concludes that his
failure to take his father's advice was the true cause of all his
misfortunes. "If we do not allow a visible Curse to pursue visible
Crimes," he moralizes, "how shall we reconcile the Events of
Things with the Divine Justice?" (II, 181). Certainly Crusoe's
entire narrative is based upon the assumption that God is continually punishing him for his "original sin."

After his first shipwreck the captain warns Crusoe never to
voyage again, for it was obviously against the "visible Hand of
Heaven." And when Crusoe angrily asks him whether *he* will
continue to go to sea, the captain replies, "That is another Case
. . . *it is my Calling, and therefore my Duty*" (I, 15). Crusoe rejects this
advice, embarking once more as a passenger. On this voyage he
gains neither wealth nor experience, and he is barely saved from
joining the navy as a common sailor by a friend who offers to take
him to Africa. This time he learns the art of sailing in addition to
earning some money as a merchant, but even on this trip he falls
sick of a calenture. When he ventures again, he is captured by the
Moors and made a slave at Sallee, where he is forced to suffer all
the humiliations suggested by his father's "prophetick Discourse"
(I, 20). Here he has the leisure to contemplate the rewards of his sin.
His punishment always seems to take the form of physical labor,
which symbolizes his decline from the middle class.

Crusoe eventually escapes from this manual toil as a gardener
and a fisherman, but the price is a return to the very station of life
which he was trying to avoid. Brought to Brazil, he becomes a
planter and achieves the comfort of the "middle station" in which
God seems determined to place him. But Crusoe is not happy. "I
was gotten into an Employment quite remote to my Genius," he
tells the reader, "and directly contrary to the Life I delighted in,
and for which I forsook my Father's House, and broke thro' all his
good Advice; nay, I was coming into the very Middle Station, or
Upper Degree of low Life, which my Father advised me to before;

and which if I resolved to go on with, I might ha' staid at Home . . ." (I, 39). During his four years in Brazil, Crusoe's wealth increases enormously. His plantation grows and he has several servants as well as a slave. Thus Crusoe's decision to leave his plantation is an indication of his restlessness, but it is hardly the restlessness of the enterprising businessman.[28] Certainly his decision to enter the slave trade is part of a desire to acquire wealth, but Crusoe's real motive is his renewed desire to travel. On the island, shipwrecked and alone, he confesses that his condition is the result of God's punishment upon him for leaving his plantation and the calling in which he might have been prosperous, if neither content nor happy. The result of this folly is once more to be thrown from the pleasures of the "middle station" into "the miseries and Hardships, the Labour and Sufferings of the mechanick Part of Mankind" (I, 2).

Unless we understand how much Crusoe suffers in his twenty-eight years of isolation, it will be impossible to understand why he regards himself as an exemplar of God's revenge upon the man who leaves his calling. Since Rousseau's eulogy of Crusoe's life in *Émile*, many critics have regarded the island as a do-it-yourself utopia. Of course Crusoe takes what satisfaction he can find in his attempts to re-create the products of European civilization. But Defoe's hero is not a hermit by nature; he survives his solitude, but he does not enjoy it. When in his prayers Crusoe is about to thank God for giving him happiness, he reproaches himself for lying: "I know not what it was, but something shock'd my Mind at that Thought, and I durst not speak the Words: How canst thou be such a Hypocrite,

---

[28] The difference between the conservative mercantilist businessman and the capitalist is best seen in Bernard Mandeville's distinction between "Diligence" and "Industry." Mandeville argued that a man might be hard-working and save his money without thinking of improving his station in life, whereas "Industry implies, besides the other Qualities, a Thirst after Gain; and an indefatigable Desire of meliorating our Condition." Crusoe's father is diligent but not industrious, whereas his son has neither of these qualities. See Mandeville, *The Fable of the Bees*, ed. F. B. Kaye (Oxford, 1924), I, 244.

(said I, even audibly) to pretend to be thankful for a Condition, which however thou may'st endeavour to be contented with, thou would'st rather pray heartily to be deliver'd from" (I, 131). For all the pleasure he finds in invention, he never regards his labor as anything but a humiliating punishment for his sin.

Crusoe is explicit concerning the moral that can be drawn from his sufferings in his longing for companionship and his terror at the prospect of being devoured by cannibals.

> I have been in all my Circumstances a *Memento* to those who are touched with the general Plague of Mankind, whence for ought I know one half of their Miseries flow; I mean, that of not being satisfied with the station wherein God and Nature has plac'd them; for not to look back upon my primitive Condition . . . and the excellent Advice of my Father, the Opposition to which, was, *as I may call it,* my ORIGINAL SIN; my subsequent Mistakes of the same Kind had been the Means of my coming into this miserable Condition. (I, 225)

Crusoe feels that his story should teach content to those "who cannot enjoy comfortably what God has given them" (I, 150). It has been argued that the real moral turns on Crusoe's success in the world, but there is no reason to believe that he would not have been as rich if he had not left York. It is certain that he would have been wealthier if he had remained in Brazil to cultivate his garden.[29]

[29] Although it is futile to speculate on Crusoe's possible success as a lawyer or a tradesman in England, there is no reason to assume that he gains materially by his wandering. There is, however, no question that he loses money by his stay on the island. Reckoning his prospects in Brazil, he states that he would have been a rich man had he remained on his plantation, "for had that Providence, which so happily had seated me at the *Brasils*, as a Planter, bless'd me with confin'd Desires, and I could have been contented to have gone on gradually, I might have been by this Time; *I mean in the Time of my being in this Island*, one of the most considerable Planters in the *Brasils*, nay, I am perswaded, that by the Improvements I had made, in that little Time I liv'd there, and the Encrease I should probably have made, if I had stay'd, I might have been worth an hundred thousand *Moydors* [£137,500] . . . " (I, 225). Crusoe receives some returns from his plantation, but most of his annual profit has gone to the monastery of Saint Augustine where it is used for charity and the conversion of the Indians. He emerges from his experience moderately wealthy, but not rich.

After his many years on the island, Crusoe might be expected to have learned the contentment that he preaches to his readers. Happily married, with three children and a comfortable income, Crusoe nevertheless has a sudden desire to return to his island. But for the first time in his life he succeeds in conquering his wandering spirit by purchasing a farm. Now Crusoe believes that he is finally following his father's wishes and adapting himself to the "middle State of Life" (II, 116). In reality, however, Crusoe has not come to terms with the mercantile world, for he tries to re-create the independent life of his island in the middle of England. "I farm'd my own Land," he boasts; "I had no rent to pay, was limited by no Articles; I could pull up or cut down as I pleased: What I planted was for my self, and what I improv'd was for my Family" (II, 116). It is not surprising that his career as a "meer Country Gentleman" is short-lived. After the tragic deaths of his wife and children, Crusoe finds that he is unable to accept the middle-class illusion of content. He sees that outside his self-subsisting economic island lie the vices and the luxuries of the rich and the drudgery of the poor "in daily Strugglings for Bread to maintain the vital Strength they labour'd with, so living in a daily Circulation of Sorrow" (II, 117). Incapable of adapting himself to the ideals of his father and yet unable to endure idleness, *"the very Dregs of Life"* (II, 119), Crusoe embarks for his island once more.

To return to his island as its governor, to use his wealth in promoting the welfare of its settlers, would have been the new calling that God had chosen for Crusoe. This is indicated both by the intensity of his obsession about returning to the island, which his wife believed was "some secret powerful Impulse of Providence" (II, 114), and by his lack of success in England. But Crusoe rejects his responsibility again, and after establishing laws for the colony and sending supplies from Brazil, he sets off on his travels. "I was possesst with a wandering Spirit," says Crusoe, and he adds a warning: "Let no wise Man flatter himself, with the Strength of his own Judgment, as if he was able to chuse any particular Station of Life for himself: Man is a short-sighted Creature, sees but a very

little Way before him; and as his Passions, are none of his best
Friends, so his particular Affections are generally his worst Counsel-
lors" (III, 81). Crusoe's choice of a "Station" is not a calling but
merely a desire to travel. In deciding to leave his island for the last
time, Crusoe remarks that he "scorn'd all Advantages" (III, 80),
and his disregard of his own interests produces the usual result. He
is punished once more, this time by being abandoned by his
mutinous crew at Bengal. Here, as we have seen, he enters business
only to quit this prosperous way of life in order to make the
dangerous voyage back to England through Siberia.

At the beginning of his *Serious Reflections*, Crusoe contrasts the folly
of the desert fathers with the wisdom of an acquaintance, a poor
laborer, who followed his calling, led a pious life, and achieved a
sufficient degree of solitude in the midst of society.[30] The Puritan, as
William Haller remarks, "had no reason to fear the world or run
away from it. Rather he must go forth and do the will of God
there." [31] Unlike his own example of the religious laborer or
Haller's puritan saint, Crusoe is continually running from his
world. He views his story as a struggle between his reason, which
tells him to follow his calling, and his triumphant passions, which
force him to wander. On his island he is converted to an active
Christianity and recognizes that God is punishing him for his
transgressions, but "poor, wicked" Robinson Crusoe sins in spite of
his religious faith. He has unquestionable powers of industry and
invention, but any view of Crusoe as the embodiment of the
capitalistic spirit or as economic man must take into account his
penchant for traveling and his hatred of a steady life. Crusoe does
not disobey his parents in the name of free enterprise or economic
freedom, but for a strangely adventurous, romantic, and unprofit-

[30] P. 13. Defoe was merely embellishing the familiar parable of Saint Anthony
and the tailor, which was frequently used to recommend contentment in one's
calling and to attack monasticism. Cf. Richard Steele, *The Tradesman's Calling*
(London, 1684), pp. 213–215, where the characters are a hermit and a cobbler,
with the original legend in *The Sayings of the Fathers*, in *The Paradise or Garden of the
Holy Fathers*, trans, Wallis Budge (London, 1907), pp. 149–150.
[31] *The Rise of Puritanism* (New York, 1957), p. 123.

able desire to see foreign lands. If any economic moral can be drawn from Crusoe's narrative, it is a conservative warning that Englishmen about to embark on the economic disaster of the South Sea Bubble should mind their callings and stick to the sure road of trade.

Robinson Crusoe's Conversion

by George A. Starr

1. Crusoe's "Original Sin"

Crusoe's running away to sea has long intrigued readers. Within months of the book's original appearance, Defoe's treatment of the incident was challenged: Charles Gildon was the first to object that Defoe presents as sinful a deed which seems at worst a mild offense, if not altogether justifiable, and that he ascribes to it consequences which seem out of all proportion to its gravity, even if one were to grant its culpability.[1] Modern commentators react less indignantly than Gildon, but they continue to feel that Defoe's handling of the matter requires explanation. Both Crusoe's motivation in leaving home, and Defoe's reason for labelling the act a sin, have been variously interpreted in recent years.

According to Maximillian Novak, "the rationale for this action may be found in Crusoe's personal characteristics: his lack of economic prudence, his inability to follow a steady profession, his indifference to a calm bourgeois life, and his love of travel."[2] In stressing these "personal characteristics," however, Mr. Novak, it seems to me, reads into the account a rather more individualized

"Robinson Crusoe's Conversion." Selections from "Robinson Crusoe," in G. A. Starr, *Defoe & Spiritual Autobiography* (copyright © 1965 by Princeton University Press), pp. 74–123 [notes 13–22 renumbered]. Reprinted by permission of Princeton University Press. All references to Defoe's fiction are to the edition by George A. Aitken cited in the bibliography of this book.

[1] *The Life and Strange Surprizing Adventures of Mr. D. . . . . De F . . . of London, Hosier . . .* (1719); edited by Paul Dottin as *Robinson Crusoe Examin'd and Criticis'd . . .* (London and Paris, 1923), pp. 82–87.

[2] *Economics and the Fiction of Daniel Defoe* (Berkeley and Los Angeles, 1962), p. 32.

portrait than Defoe actually gives us at this stage of the book. Four years before the appearance of *Robinson Crusoe*, Defoe had assessed the temperament of youth as follows: *"Folly that is bound up in the Heart of a Child,* says Solomon, *is driven by the Rod of Correction. . . . What this folly is,* needs no Description here, other than an allow'd Custom in doing Evil, a natural Propensity we all have to Evil; with this we are all born into the world, the Soul is originally bent to Folly." [3] In the last book he wrote, Defoe was to observe that "men are in their youth hurry'd down the stream of their worst affeccions by the meer insensible impetuosity of nature." [4] The motives he imputes to Robinson Crusoe do not, I think, amount to more than this. That man is naturally subject to rebellious impulse is a principle he frequently asserts, and it would appear to provide a sufficient "rationale" for Crusoe's behavior on this occasion. Indeed, the episode seems to rest on an orthodox Calvinistic conception of man's innate waywardness and obstinacy. Obadiah Grew, an ejected Presbyterian minister like those under whom Defoe was educated, expresses the traditional belief in his assertion that "every man by nature hath a lusting desire to leave God, and live at his own hand; he would stand on his own legs and bottom, and be at his own dispose: Thus it is with every man by Nature . . . Man

---

[3] *Family Instructor,* I, 68. Compare *Mere Nature Delineated; Or, A Body without a Soul* (1726), in which Defoe asks, "why does Meer Nature lead to foolish Things by the Course of its own Instinct? Why hurry the Soul down the Stream of his Affections, and, with inexpressible Gust, to what is gross, sordid, and brutish, whereas Wisdom and virtuous Principles are all up Hill, against the Stream, and are rather acquir'd than natural? Let those who deny original Depravity, answer this for me, if they think they can; for my Part, I acknowledge it to be out of my Reach, upon any other foot" (p. 44). In *Religious Courtship* Defoe similarly declares that "nature prompts us to evil thoughts and evil desires, and to them only; the imagination of the thoughts of our hearts are evil, and only evil; if there are any good motions, or heavenly desires in the heart, they are from God" (p. 55).

[4] *The Compleat English Gentleman,* edited by K. D. Bülbring (1890), p. 111. Cf. also *Serious Reflections,* pp. 104, 267; *Review,* Nov. 4, 1704, edited in facsimile by Arthur W. Secord, 22 vols. (N.Y., 1938), I, 294; *Little Review,* June 22, 1705, pp. 21-22; *A New Discovery of an Old Intreague: A Satyr levell'd at Treachery and Ambition,* in *A Second Volume of the Writings of the Author of the True-Born Englishman* (1705), p. 19. H. H. Andersen discusses the matter in "The Paradox of Trade and Morality in Defoe," *MP,* xxxix (1941), pp. 29, 43.

would be at liberty from God and his Will, to follow and fulfill his own; *Man is born like a wild Asses Colt;* vain man is so, saith *Zophar*. He hath a *principium laesum*, a devillish principle in his nature; an impulse to range about the earth, as Satan said of himself." [5] Crusoe's father admonishes him "not to play the young man," and a generalized portrait of the young man as "wild Asses Colt" is, in effect, what we are given at the outset, rather than individual traits.[6] On this reading, then, Crusoe is motivated by the wildness that Defoe found characteristic of unregenerate man in general, and of youth in particular, rather than the "personal characteristics" suggested by Mr. Novak.

Mr. Novak further maintains that Crusoe's sin consists in "his refusal to follow the 'calling' chosen for him by his father"; Cotton Mather and Richard Norwood are cited in support of the view that Crusoe's action violates this specific "religious-economic doctrine." [7] By drawing attention to a religious implication of the deed, Mr. Novak's study provides a useful caveat against exclusively economic interpretations.[8] But his own argument is weakened, it seems to me,

[5] *Meditations Upon our Saviour's Parable of the Prodigal Son* (1678), pp. 44, 46; cf. John Goodman, *The Penitent Pardoned*, p. 85; Ezekiel Hopkins, *Works*, p. 525.

[6] What Mr. Novak describes in positive terms as "a love of travel" should perhaps be regarded merely as Crusoe's initial manifestation of the impulse Grew deplores. Similarly, his "inability to follow a steady profession" and his "indifference to a calm bourgeois life" may be viewed as incidental effects of this inborn and universal tendency, rather than "personal characteristics." One has similar reservations about his suggested "lack of economic prudence": it may be one corollary of his *principium laesum*, but it is hard to see in what sense it is a trait of personality that contributes to his running away.

[7] *Economics* . . . , pp. 32, 40 and *passim*. On the concept of the calling, see Max Weber, *The Protestant Ethic and The Spirit of Capitalism* (N.Y., 1958), pp. 79f., 161f.; and R. H. Tawney, *Religion and The Rise of Capitalism* (N.Y., 1963), pp. 199–202.

[8] Ian Watt, for instance, maintains that Crusoe runs away "for the classic reason of *homo economicus*—that it is necessary to better his economic condition." It is "economic individualism," according to Watt, that "prevents Crusoe from paying much heed to the ties of family." As he points out, Crusoe reflects that "there seemed to be something fatal in that propension of nature" which overruled these family ties; nevertheless Watt regards the episode as the first instance of that economic motivation which he finds actuating Crusoe throughout the book. See *The Rise of the Novel* (Berkeley and Los Angeles, 1957), pp. 65, 66 and *passim*.

by narrowing Crusoe's sin to a violation of this particular doctrine. Implicit in Defoe's treatment of the episode is a conventional identification of family, social and divine order, all of which are flouted by Crusoe's deed. Since human affairs are governed by Providence, any attempt to disrupt or elude their established pattern implies a denial of God's power and, by extension, challenges his very existence.[9] The virtual equation between paternal and divine authority is too commonplace to require discussion; it rests, of course, on the fifth commandment and on Deuteronomy 27:16, a text which Defoe uses to good effect elsewhere.[10]

It is worth glancing briefly, however, at the extraordinary interest Providence takes in the "middle station in life." Crusoe's father extolls the upper station of low life as the best state in the world and the most suited to human happiness, pointing out that "the wise man gave his testimony to this as the just standard of true felicity, when he prayed to have neither poverty nor riches." He alludes to Agur's prayer (Proverbs 30:8–9): "give me neither poverty nor riches; feed me with food convenient for me: Lest I be full, and deny thee, and say Who is the Lord? or lest I be poor, and steal, and take the name of my God in vain." This theme was a favorite with contemporary moralists,[11] and Defoe reiterates it at various points in his writings.[12] It is true that Crusoe would have been under an

---

[9] This line of argument is a commonplace in treatises on Providence: see T[homas] C[rane], *Isagoge ad Dei Providentiam: or, a Prospect of Divine Providence* (1672), pp. 507–509; Stephen Charnock, "A Treatise of Divine Providence," in *Works,* 3rd edition (1699), p. 533. Defoe makes a similar point in *Serious Reflections,* pp. 191–92.

[10] See Part II of *The Family Instructor,* p. 243, where the despairing brother is made to say, "I remember that terrible Scripture with many a Reproach upon myself, *Cursed be he that setteth light by his Father and Mother.*"

[11] See *A Supplement to the Athenian Oracle* (1706), p. 290; Lady Frances (Freke) Norton, *The Applause of Virtue* (1705), pp. 255–56; *Husbandry Spiritualized,* in the *Whole Works of the Reverend Mr. John Flavel,* 2 vols. (Glasgow, 1754), II, 169; *The Works of the Pious and Profoundly Learned Joseph Mede* (1664), pp. 167–81; *The Works of Francis Osborne, Esq.,* 8th edition (1682), pp. 514, 518, and *passim.* In *The Early Masters of English Fiction* (Lawrence, 1956), Mr. McKillop notes a further expression of this idea in a sermon by Benjamin Hoadly (p. 2).

[12] Compare *Moll Flanders,* I, 200; *Review,* III, 110a; *Compleat English Gentleman,* pp.

equal obligation to accept his lot had his father been poor or rich, a laborer or a peer. His action is made to appear all the more rash and willful, however, by the very fact that he has been placed, as his father points out, "in the middle of the two extremes, between the mean and the great." He cannot plead the ignorance or want that extenuate the misdeeds of the poor, or the forgetfulness amid excess that plagues the rich; he is neither driven by necessity nor lulled by surfeit. Since wealth and poverty are equally beset by spiritual hazards, Providence has shown a special fondness for the English middle class by sparing it the temptations into which both extremes are led. In repudiating such a blessing, Crusoe—like the Prodigal Son before him—displays no mere "lack of economic prudence," but a radical perversity and impiety.

By a single act, Crusoe thus defies the joint authority of family, society, and Providence. If we bear in mind these multiple sanctions against rebellion, the question of the intrinsic enormity of running off to sea loses its relevance. In itself, the act may be somewhat more complex than, say, eating an apple, yet each deed is significant primarily as an outward token of a spiritual state. In a sense, Crusoe's original sin does cause his later misfortunes; from another point of view, it is merely the first overt expression of a more fundamental source of trouble: the natural waywardness of every unregenerate man. It "causes" what follows in that each step towards damnation necessarily leads to the next, unless conversion intervenes: thus Crusoe's option of altering his headstrong course is renewed on several subsequent occasions, but he repeats and aggravates his initial error. The running off to sea is not, in other words, the direct cause of all later vicissitudes, but it does initiate a pattern of wrongdoing which has far-reaching consequences. To use another analogy, Jonah's running away to sea does in a sense cause his later misfortunes; that is, it largely determines the outward form of the subsequent narrative. Like Crusoe's embarkation for London,

102–103; *Serious Reflections*, p. 33f.; and especially *The Compleat English Tradesman*, 2nd edition, 2 vols. (1727), II, 193–94.

Jonah's embarkation for Tarshish proves disastrous. Yet it is Jonah's fundamental rebelliousness, not the specific form which his insubordination takes, that provokes the divine wrath.

Of both Crusoe's and Jonah's first disobedience it can be said that the outward deed expresses admirably the inward state of the hero. Both acts, along with the prodigal's departure into a far country, manage to present a spiritual condition in concrete terms. In each case the initial casting off of restraint not only sets in motion a narrative interesting in its own right but also provides a kind of "objective correlative" for the hero's turbulent, unruly spirit. Other objectifications of Crusoe's spiritual state were available; the literature of sin is rich in metaphor, and the account of Crusoe's doings prior to conversion employs a number of them, some only allusively and in passing, others more extensively as integral parts of the narrative. When certain divines came to describe the nature of sin, they gave what were in effect catalogues of such metaphors. Obadiah Sedgwick, for example, asserts that "Every sinfull man is a wandring Meteor, a very Planet on earth; he is gone from the fold, as a silly sheep; he is gone from his Fathers house, as a silly Child; he is gone out of the right path, like a silly Traveller in the Wilderness. Sin puts us into a Maze, into a Labyrinth; we go from one sin to another sin, out of one by-path into another by-path; and the further we go in sinfull paths, the more still we go out of the way." [13]

As preceding chapters have shown, it was quite common for spiritual autobiographers to weave such motifs into their recollections, in order to illustrate the nature and extent of their sinfulness prior to conversion. In *Robinson Crusoe* Defoe develops such motifs to the point that they become the very fabric of his narrative. Although they take on a vitality of their own in the process, they nevertheless retain their original and basic metaphorical function.

[13] *Parable of the Prodigal*, p. 236.

2. *Crusoe Errant*

* * *

I have spoken of several gradual processes in this portion of the book—gradual alienation from God, gradual loss of control over events, gradual hardening—and it is worth looking more closely at their progressive or cumulative character. What happens is that Crusoe reaches his lowest spiritual ebb not at the time of committing his "original sin" but just before conversion. It may seem paradoxical to maintain that he embodies a conventional progression in sin. What new sins does he commit? Is not his sense of sin (when it does emerge) in excess of the actual number and enormity of his misdeeds? Part of an answer to such questions has been suggested already: if he does not repeat his dramatic violation of the fifth commandment, or learn to break any of the latter five, he nevertheless does in effect flout the first more and more boldly. It is true, in other words, that he does not sin against the paternal or social order after first running away, but his defiance of divine order becomes a settled pattern of action. Writers on habitual sin maintained not only that one sin tends to lead to other and greater sins unless repentance intervenes, but also that failure to repent for a past sin is equivalent, in terms of the welfare of one's soul, to the actual commission of new sins.[14] Thus even if each rejection of a Providential call to conversion did not constitute a new sin, Crusoe's later sense of sinfulness would be justified by his prolonged failure to repent of the single, initial sin. In fact, however, he is culpable on both counts, for divines were emphatic in condemning what one of them calls "a daring contradiction to Providence, or a bold venturing on in sin, notwithstanding the vertual-wooings and warning-knocks of Providence to the contrary."[15] The "bold

[14] See Jeremy Taylor, *Unum Necessarium*, in his *Works*, VII, 152, 159–60; cf. also Defoe, *Due Preparations for the Plague*, p. 144.

[15] T[homas] C[rane], *Isagoge* . . . , pp. 507–508; cf. Andrew Trebeck, *Sermons on Several Occasions* (1713), p. 113.

venturing on" not only allows past sin to take firmer hold, but is sinful in itself, so that the guilt is compounded.

Turning to the actual details of this process in Crusoe's case, we may begin by recalling the resemblance to Balaam mentioned earlier. Like Crusoe, Balaam ventures forth on a mission contrary to his clear duty; like Crusoe, his way is opposed by God, but he is blind to the cause of the obstacles, and persists obstinately on his course. As with Crusoe, only the appearance of an angel, brandishing a sword and threatening his destruction, finally forces him to repent. What I wish to draw attention to here is not the outward similarity between, for instance, the two visions of armed, avenging angels, but the inward affinity between the spiritual plights of Balaam and Crusoe. In each case journeying bodily is a graphic representation of erring spiritually; in both cases the ways of sin are repeatedly obstructed, and ultimately blocked altogether, in order to deflect the culprit from his false object and restore him to the true path.

Various Biblical and classical analogues to this process were available to preachers of the period. Obadiah Sedgwick says that God sometimes tries to reclaim erring man "*by a most perfect beleagring* (as it were) *of a projecting sinner:* hedging up all his ways with thorns, or immuring him as in a Castle, and shutting of him up, that there shall be no going out or coming in." [16] Seen in these terms, Crusoe's arrival on the island marks yet another more drastic stage in God's efforts to reclaim him. It is at once the most dramatic of his long series of deliverances, and the most effective barrier to his persistent vagabondage. The shipwreck is meant to halt his erring career and to awaken him to a new life; what happens, however, is that only his outward circumstances change. Initially, to be sure, he is struck by his escape, but his elation soon gives way to despair, for, as he records in his journal, "instead of being thankful to God for my

---

[16] *Parable of the Prodigal*, p. 64; cf. Hosea 2:6, "Therefore, behold, I will hedge up thy way with thorns, and make a wall, that she shall not find her paths." Cf. also Ryther, *Plat for Mariners*, pp. 30–31; [Richard Allestree], *The Causes of The Decay of Christian Piety* (1677), p. 180.

deliverance . . . I ran about the shore, wringing my hands, and beating my head and face, exclaiming at my misery, and crying out, I was undone, undone" (p. 75). When he does regain his composure, he once again fails to interpret the personal significance of what he has just experienced.

On the one hand, the brief ecstasy, as he later calls it, "ended where it began, in a mere common flight of joy," without leading to any "reflection upon the distinguished goodness of the hand which had preserved me," or any "inquiry why Providence had been thus merciful to me." On the other hand, he later acknowledges that as soon as he saw he was not doomed to starve, "all the sense of my affliction wore off . . . [I] was far enough from being afflicted at my condition, as a judgment from heaven, or as the hand of God against me" (p. 98). Regarded *either* as a deliverance or as an affliction, this episode might have taken effect, but in fact the Providential design in it is frustrated, and it takes its place among the calls to repentance which go unheeded. In terms of Crusoe's spiritual state, it marks yet another slight of the "vertual-wooings and warning-knocks of Providence"; like Balaam, he goes mulishly on, although "by a most perfect beleagring (as it were)" the way of the "projecting sinner" is now hedged up with thorns. Thus the arrival at the island may be less of a turning point than is generally supposed: a new beginning in only a qualified sense, it is more basically an extension of a pattern of action initiated by the embarkation at Hull.

Two important episodes between Crusoe's landing on the island and his conversion are discussed in the Appendix—namely the springing up of the barley, and the earthquake. In light of the foregoing discussion, it should be clear why Crusoe later singles out these two incidents, among all those between his landing and his sickness, for special regretful comment. Like the events just considered, they again display Providence's concern for him and power over him; they again invite him (once gently, once harshly) to repent; but they again fail to take effect. Rather than dwelling further here on their significance, we shall find it more fruitful to turn directly to the climactic episode of this long series: Crusoe's illness.

It was of course traditional to represent spiritual infirmity through bodily disease, to express God's cure of souls in medical metaphors, and to regard actual sickness as a particularly opportune occasion for setting repentance in motion.[17] Seen against such a background, Crusoe's malady is another striking instance of Defoe's ability to exploit fully the narrative possibilities of commonplace events, and at the same time to avail himself of their conventional spiritual significance. Thus the chart of Crusoe's case history, which he is made to record in his journal (pp. 95–96), has a thoroughly clinical verisimilitude; this gives the dream and its consequences a plausibility which they might have lacked had they come, for instance, in a season of callous, bustling prosperity. More fundamentally, however, Crusoe's sickness and dream serve as final indications of the spiritual condition which he has reached, and of the greatness of the change he is about to undergo. These effects are achieved partly, as already noted, by the overt resemblance between this stern apparition and certain Biblical ones. But they are also owing in part to the tradition of hardy sinners bowed by sickness. Without recapitulating earlier discussion of such motifs in spiritual autobiographies, or citing any further evidence of their prevalence in homiletic and practical works, we may recall that they appear very early in the literature of conversion. As one of Defoe's contemporaries obligingly pointed out to his parishioners, "not only by outward Means, but by immediate Operations and Impressions, and those, very sensible, strong, and lively, have the Convictions of some Men been wrought in them. Of all which, St. *Austin* is a most remarkable Instance, who in his *Confessions* (a Book I think translated into English and worthy your Perusal) hath recorded the many Warnings he had from God, by his own

---

[17] The first two ideas are elaborated by William Hopkins in *A Sermon Preached . . . September 3, 1683*, pp. 15–16; for the third, see Philip Doddridge, *Practical Discourse of Regeneration*, in *Works*, 10 vols. (Leeds, 1803), I, 507; Tillotson, "Of the End of Judgments, and the Reason of their Continuance," in *Works*, I, 192, 194.

Sickness; the Death of his Companions in Sin; the overruling Providences of God; the inward Motions, and Convictions of his own Conscience; and at last by a *Voice* from Heaven; commanding him to take up the Bible, and read." [18]

The preceding examination of Crusoe's adventures after embarking at Hull has shown that besides merely leading him to the island by plausible stages, they function as "the many Warnings" which he, like Augustine, "had from God," and that their sequence is completed not with the arrival at the island but at the point of conversion. The fact that nothing less drastic than the appearance of an avenging angel will serve to awaken Crusoe indicates how grave his spiritual malady has become, yet at the same time enhances the importance of his conversion and heightens the attainments possible to him through regeneration. Earlier chapters have discussed the trait, so common to spiritual autobiographers, of magnifying one's ultimate condition by contrasting it with what preceded conversion. Regarded in these terms, Crusoe's vicissitudes magnify the scope, the patience, and the benevolence of Providence; his conversion, however, magnifies not only the abundance of grace to the sinner, but also, by implication, the potential stature of the ex-sinner himself. It was said of the Puritan worthy Robert Bolton that "it pleased God to bring him to repentance, but by such a way as the Lord seldom useth, but upon such strong vessels, as he intendeth for strong encounters, and rare employments; for the Lord ranne upon him as a Giant, taking him by the neck, and shaking him to pieces, as he did *Iob;* beating him to the ground as he did *Paul,* by laying before him the ugly visage of his sins, which lay so heavy upon him that he roared for anguish of heart." [19] It is in this tradition that Defoe places Crusoe, by investing his conversion with such grand agents as a fire-clad, spear-brandishing apparition. . . .

[18] Waple, *Thirty Sermons,* p. 395.
[19] Samuel Clarke, *The Marrow of Ecclesiastical History,* 2nd edition (1654), p. 925.

3. Conversion and Regeneration

* * *

Crusoe's relations with Friday deserve particular attention because they supply yet another test of the importance of religious concerns to the book's total structure. Like the running away to sea and various events that follow, Friday's role has been discussed by one recent critic mainly in economic terms. His rescue merely marks "the advent of new manpower"; Crusoe's dealings with him are altogether egocentric; communication between them is strictly utilitarian, so that "A functional silence, broken only by an occasional 'No, Friday,' or an abject 'Yes, Master,' is the golden music of Crusoe's *île joyeuse.*" [20]

While it cannot be denied that Friday's arrival results in new planting and building, it is surely an error to regard this as its sole, or even its main implication. We have seen that a constant feature of spiritual autobiographies, and indeed a primary motive in their very composition, is the urge to impart to others the benefits of one's own conversion; we have also noted that the growth of this didactic impulse is a phenomenon recognized and endorsed by writers on regeneration other than autobiographers. On the one hand, to have experienced conversion oneself was regarded as a necessary qualification for evangelizing, and on the other, it was felt that genuine conversion naturally gives rise to a kind of missionary zeal. [21] It is this aspect of Crusoe's relations with Friday that seems most striking, for after being "called plainly by Providence to save this

---

[20] *The Rise of the Novel*, pp. 73, 69. Immediately before alleging this "functional silence," Mr. Watt quotes the following remark of Crusoe's, omitting what I have italicized: "*the conversation which employed the hours between Friday and I was such, as made the three years which we lived there together* perfectly and completely happy, if any such thing as complete happiness can be formed in a sublunary state." "Conversation" is the subject of the sentence: through its omission, Crusoe's meaning is reversed.

[21] In *The Farther Adventures of Robinson Crusoe*, the French priest declares that "true religion is naturally communicative, and he that is once made a Christian will never leave a pagan behind him if he can help it" (p. 145).

poor creature's life" (p. 225), Crusoe becomes the Providential agent of his rescue from paganism.

Just as Crusoe had discovered for himself the essentials of Christianity by reading the Bible, contemplating the works of nature, and reflecting on his own experience, so his indoctrination of Friday provides a second demonstration of the simplicity and reasonableness of such belief as is necessary to salvation. Moreover, his guidance of Friday displays the progress of Crusoe's own regeneration, in that he now learns to expound and defend his faith. It is true that he is posed by several of Friday's ingenuous questions, and he acknowledges that "I was but a young doctor, and ill enough qualified for a casuist, or a solver of difficulties. . . . I had, God knows, more sincerity than knowledge in all the methods I took for this poor creature's instruction" (pp. 243, 45). But this confession, too, besides lending plausibility in the same way as do his awkward improvisations in other spheres, is part of the traditional conception of the fledgling spiritual guide. As was shown earlier, the lay convert was encouraged to share his discoveries with others not only for the good it might do them but for the value it must have to himself. In Chapter I we saw the double function— didactic and autodidactic—ascribed throughout the period to spiritual autobiography in particular, and to the exchange of religious knowledge and experience in general. Here the principle is made quite explicit, in Crusoe's declaration that "in laying things open to him, I really informed and instructed myself in many things that either I did not know, or had not fully considered before, but which occurred naturally to my mind upon my searching into them for the information of this poor savage. And I had more affection in my inquiry after things upon this occasion than ever I felt before; so that whether this poor wild wretch was the better for me or no, I had great reason to be thankful that ever he came to me." [22] In short, communication between Crusoe and Friday is "utilitarian"

---

[22] P. 245; cf. *The Farther Adventures*, p. 142, where it is said of Will Atkins that "when he comes to talk religion to his wife, he will talk himself effectually into it; for attempting to teach others is sometimes the best way of teaching ourselves."

in a sense quite different from that which Mr. Watt has in mind. It is useful not to one party but to both, and it is useful not so much for the exploitation of new manpower—signs, effective enough at first, would have remained sufficient for that—as for the salvation of one soul and the growth of another.

Besides becoming Friday's spiritual mentor, Crusoe is also his master, and a further point should be made about this aspect of their relationship. Prior to his conversion, Crusoe rebels against divine authority, yet his attempt to become independent results in an actual loss of mastery over himself and his circumstances. Eventually, through submitting to God and acknowledging his dependence upon Providence, he in fact acquires a new degree of control over his environment, and over himself as well. In seeking to be a law unto himself, he had lost the power that was properly his; in surrendering to the sovereignty of Providence, he gains extraordinary powers. In any case, it seems legitimate to regard his mastery over Friday in this light, as made possible by his own submission to God, and as a further embodiment of a paradox running throughout the book: that sinful independence results in Crusoe's enslavement, both literal and figurative, while virtuous dependence issues in mastery, again literal and figurative.

The paradox might also be stated in terms of the relation between parent and child. In the early part of the book Crusoe virtually orphans himself through disobedience: in challenging the authority of a father he loses the security of a son. But through humbling himself towards his other Father, and reassuming the dutifulness of a son, Crusoe paradoxically gains parental power himself, since his relations with Friday are in large part those of father to child, as he himself declares (p. 232). Thus the parent-child motif further illustrates the nature and extent of the change that Crusoe undergoes. . . .

The Conclusion of *Robinson Crusoe*

by J. Paul Hunter

The adventure plot of *Robinson Crusoe* has often been critically discussed, but this plot takes on far greater significance when viewed in relation to the novel's thematic concerns. Crusoe's physical activities relate to his spiritual life not only because conversion alters his conduct; throughout *Robinson Crusoe* physical events reflect Crusoe's spiritual state, for Crusoe is concerned with accommodating himself to his world spiritually and physically at the same time, and his efforts to come to terms with his physical environment parallel his efforts to find a proper relationship with his God. Ultimately, his physical activities become a metaphor for his spiritual aspirations.

Defoe has constructed *Robinson Crusoe* so that its theme gives survival an added dimension. Man, placed in a primitive context, faces not only a physical world that is hostile, but a world where he is spiritually an alien; he has to fight not only the physical dangers of storms, hunger, sickness, wild beasts, and cannibals, but temptation, moral evil, and ultimately (because man's nature has become depraved) even himself—all on the single island battleground of his life.

Emphasis upon the "realistic" nature of both Defoe's choice of detail and his use of language has obscured the emblematic

"The Conclusion of *Robinson Crusoe*." Excerpted from *The Reluctant Pilgrim: Defoe's Emblematic Method and Quest for Form in Robinson Crusoe*, by J. Paul Hunter (Baltimore: Johns Hopkins University Press, 1966), pp. 188–201. Reprinted by permission of Johns Hopkins University Press. References to *Robinson Crusoe* are taken from the Shakespeare Head edition (Oxford, 1927–28); volumes are cited as A and B.

meaning of Crusoe's physical activities, but Defoe's "realism" is like that of Bunyan and substantiates the metaphor, rather than weakening it. Defoe, like Bunyan,[1] continually makes his hero express his spiritual condition by physical actions. The fusion of physical and spiritual concerns is implicit throughout *Robinson Crusoe*, and the general pattern of Crusoe's action is emblematic of larger matters. Crusoe's erratic straying from his course at sea, his Turkish slavery, and his shipwreck upon the rocks parallel his spiritual drift, his bondage to sin, and the "spiritual shipwreck" (to use the standard term of the guide tradition) of his soul, just as his island deliverance presages his being set apart and his relief from sickness parallels the cure of his soul. Similarly, his efforts to convert the island wilderness into a garden parallel his efforts to cultivate his spiritual self, weeding out the wild undergrowth of desires which, since man's fall, "naturally" choke the life of the soul.

Individual episodes also reflect Defoe's emblematic view of events and human actions. Crusoe's efforts to sustain himself physically from the wrecked ship, for example, parallel his efforts to obtain God's grace, according to the contemporary Puritan view: Crusoe must venture to the ship as best he can, once God has providentially intervened to bring it within his reach. Similarly, Defoe has Crusoe discover the miraculous "straggling Stalks" of grain beside his habitation and notes his first religious promptings which, though brief, are gradually multiplied by nurture and care, like his crop of grain. Later, his first physical act of kindness for Friday presages his subsequent spiritual aid: "I gave him Bread," reports Crusoe, "and a Bunch of Raisins to eat, and a Draught of Water . . ." (A238). Crusoe's attacks of "falling-sickness" are also indicated emblematically. His discovery of the terrifying footprint indicates that not all

---

[1] When meeting Faithful, for example, Christian rushes to catch up with him and "did also overrun him; so the last was first." "Then," reports Bunyan, "did Christian vaingloriously smile, because he had gotten the start of his brother; but not taking good heed to his feet, he suddenly stumbled and fell . . ." (*The Pilgrim's Progress*, ed. James Blanton Wharey, rev. Roger Sharrock [2d ed.; Oxford, 1960], p. 66).

is as perfect as the complacent Crusoe had thought, that still to be conquered are enemies not yet dreamed of in Crusoe's philosophy.[2] And his meanders in the canoe, when he comes close to taking deliverance into his own hands, emblematize his spiritual drift from his course of total reliance on God—a drift which, like one of his excursions, is almost fatal because the natural current is so strong that it can scarcely be resisted.

The language of *Robinson Crusoe* is also carefully calculated to suggest the fusion of physical and spiritual. In his feverish sickness, Crusoe describes his physical condition in terms which exactly express his spiritual aspirations just before conversion. "I was," he reports, "ready to perish for Thirst, but so weak, I had not Strength to stand up, or to get my self any Water to drink" (A99); later, after a brief prayer for mercy and then a deep sleep (but before his prayer of repentance), he finds himself "much refresh'd, but weak, and exceeding thirsty . . ." (A99–100). Such verbal ambiguity, implicit in the first third of the novel, becomes explicit at the time of Crusoe's conversion, when he for the first time becomes conscious of the potentiality of words. Previously, his interpretation of "deliverance" had been purely physical, but now he begins to "construe the Words . . . in a different sense from what I had ever done before," and his physical deliverance becomes secondary, though it remains emblematic of his spiritual deliverance.

It is in this context that we may most profitably examine the novel's last major episode, the attack by wolves in the Pyrenees. This episode has been condemned severely as unnecessary and anticlimactic, an example of Defoe's pandering to popular taste, his careless craftsmanship, and his inability to provide unity of action. Viewed in relation to Crusoe's maturation and the novel's emblematic method, however, the episode takes on significant meaning and provides a dramatic climax to the previous physical and spiritual adventures.

----

[2] Though Crusoe is intellectually aware of man's depravity, the idea has no real meaning for him until his personal confrontation with "natural" men—the cannibals.

During his stay on the island, Crusoe matures in important ways. His progress is not uniform, for certain events (such as the finding of the footprint) disrupt his composure and interrupt his development toward self-knowledge and self-control, but after conversion he clarifies his relationship to his environment and gains increasing control over himself and his world. He comes to think of himself as a "general," and as "monarch" and "governor" of his island, and he develops increasing confidence in his ability to conquer his environment and to lead men. It is particularly in the final years that Crusoe demonstrates his self-assurance and leadership ability. To Friday, he becomes both tutor and master, Christianizing and civilizing the natural savage and then ordering their combined lives rationally and responsibly. Soon God "directs" Crusoe to organized action as the cannibal barbarians prepare to destroy the life of a Christian captive—a Spaniard who had been captured after a shipwreck near another island.[3] Crusoe conducts the rescue coolly and methodically, with the finesse of a military leader but with the zeal of a crusader. "As soon as the first Shot was made," reports Crusoe, "I threw down the Piece, and took up the Fowling-Piece, and *Friday* did the like; he see me cock, and present, he did the same again; Are you ready? *Friday*, said I; Yes says he; let fly then, says I, in the Name of God, and with that I fir'd again among the amaz'd Wretches and so did *Friday* . . ." (B22). With the Spaniard rescued and Friday's father along with him,[4] Crusoe now finds his island population expanded to four, and his leadership qualities are further challenged, especially since the society is hardly a homogeneous one. "My Island," Crusoe rejoices, "was now peopled, and I thought my self very rich in Subjects; and it was a merry Reflection

---

[3] Crusoe's attack on the cannibals here is justified because the life of a Christian is at stake. His previous contemplation had guided him to leave the cannibals alone unless their existence directly impinged upon the lives of men outside their own religious tradition.

[4] The "coincidence" of the reunion of Friday and his father, like the startling coincidences in *Tom Jones*, may offend modern notions of probability, but such coincidences reflect (and dramatize) Christian assumptions about the divine control of human events.

which I frequently made, How like a King I look'd. . . . I was
absolute Lord and Lawgiver. . . . It was remarkable too, we had
but three Subjects, and they were of three different Religions. My
man *Friday* was a Protestant, his father was a *Pagan* and a *Cannibal*,
and the *Spaniard* was a Papist: However, I allow'd Liberty of
Conscience throughout my dominions . . ." (B30–31).[5]

Crusoe's first acts of leadership are clumsy and ultimately
ill-fated, for his monarchy is too absolute (note his royal "we" in the
above quotation and his messianic assumption of a divine stance),
and he tries to outplan providence. But shortly after planning to sail
away and after sending his two newest subjects to find additional
manpower, Crusoe faces a greater challenge and handles it
masterfully. Invaded by a boatload of mutineers, he first frees their
deposed captain and then conquers the mutineers, one by one, and
recruits the most likely captives under his own banner.[6] At last he
wins the sworn allegiance of all but the most incorrigible rebels, and
the ship is placed at his disposal. He is now master of himself and
an acknowledged leader of men (all his subjects call him "Gover-
nour"), but he is also conscious of the full hierarchy of command. "I
forgot not," Crusoe reports, "to lift up my Heart in Thankfulness to
. . . [God] who had not only in a miraculous Manner provided for
one in such a Wilderness, and in such a desolate Condition, but
from whom every Deliverance must always be acknowledged to
proceed" (B68).

Crusoe's full development is artistically established, however,
only when he demonstrates his mastery in the setting of the larger
world, free of the limitations of a never-never island world where he
had special rights and a special claim to leadership. Back in
Europe, but not yet permanently home, Crusoe first settles his

---

[5] Crusoe's summary is of course comic in tone, but the "Liberty of Conscience"
he allows illustrates his broadened vision of Christian social relationships.

[6] Crusoe imprisons five of the leaders in a cave. This action seems to recall
Joshua's confinement of five heathen kings in a cave (see Josh. 10:15 ff.). Defoe
may have intended the allusion to ally the mutineers' cause with a higher form of
rebellion and thus to suggest the righteousness of Crusoe's own actions.

personal affairs[7] and then, on his final journey, proves that his developed talents can stand more severe tests. He becomes "Captain" of a group of English merchants and Portuguese gentlemen who have no obligation to Crusoe; they choose him as leader solely on his merit, and he justifies their confidence by guiding them safely through a life-or-death battle.

In this last major episode Defoe again allows biblical allusion to carry the weight of meaning. Leaving Madrid by land, Crusoe's company wanders toward France but is frustrated by several delays. By "Meanders" and "winding Ways," they at last reach the mountains near Pamplona and take a prospect of the country they wish to reach. "All on a sudden," reports Crusoe, "[the guide] shew'd us the pleasant fruitful Provinces of *Languedoc* and *Gascoign,* all green and flourishing . . ." (B89).

Crusoe's view of the land he wishes to enter is the climax of a series of "prospects" in the novel. The earlier prospects, however, produce only mirages, false confidence, and unfounded hope of immediate deliverance. During his first days on the island, on a pinnacle overlooking the open sea, Crusoe buoys his hope with false imaginings. "I could not forbear," he reports, "getting up to the Top of a little Mountain and looking out to Sea in hopes of seeing a Ship, then fancy at a vast Distance I spy'd a Sail, please my self with the Hopes of it, and then after looking steadily till I was almost blind, lose it quite, and sit down and weep like a Child, and thus encrease my Misery by my Folly" (A79). Later, he twice scans the sea to observe currents so that he may calculate how to deliver himself. Another time, just after admitting that the footprint has disrupted his religious devotion and confounded his trust in God, he again thinks he sees a ship of deliverance, but the sight is "so remote, that I could not tell what to make of it" (A190), and his eyes prove too tired and weak to retain such a speck of hope. But Crusoe's final prospect—through eyes whose sight is sharpened by a

---

[7] Crusoe's handling of his estate is meticulous but unselfish. He liberally distributes his possessions to relatives, to friends, and to charity (B82–83). Cf. Jesus' charge to his disciples.

more calm, more mature spirituality—is informed by the contemporary understanding of Moses' prospect of the promised land, probably the ultimate inspiration of the seventeenth century's prospect tradition in both poetry and painting. Moses, though barred by God from entering the earthly Canaan, achieved heavenly paradise instead, and contemporary theologians regarded his prospect from Mount Nebo (atop Mount Pisgah) as a foretaste of his reward, for Canaan was a standard "type" of Heaven.[8] And modern man, according to theologians, could be inspired by similar prospects (even meditative ones) to remain on course in his pilgrimage through life.[9] "Can there be," Joseph Cooper asks in his *Misthoskopia: A Prospect of Heavenly Glory for the Comfort of Sion's Mourners* (1700), "a more cordial joy, a more entrancing delight, a more strong and everlasting consolation, than for the Soul to feed upon hidden Manna; to have the sweet and delicious Clusters of *Canaan* to refresh it in the wilderness; to dwell continually upon the

---

[8] John Flavell describes Moses' prospect and subsequent death this way: "Get thee up to Mount Nebo, saith God, and dye there, thou shalt not go over Jordan, and yet Moses was no loser by it. Though God shut him out of Canaan, he took him to heaven" (*Mount Pisgah* [London, 1689], p. 7). In seventeenth-century Puritan literature, Canaan, Jerusalem, and Sion were all metaphors for heaven.

[9] Benjamin Keach describes life's pilgrimage this way (*Tropologia: Or a Key To Open Scripture Metaphors* [London, 1681], II, 170):

> A Pilgrim in his Travels goes up-hill and down-hill; sometimes he meets with good Way, and sometimes with bad Way; Sometimes he passeth over Stiles, and through dirty Lanes; and then through green Fields and pleasant Pastures, and delightful Paths, till he comes to the desired Place.
> So the Pilgrim that would travel to the New Jerusalem, meets with various Ways and Passages. 1. He must go out of the horrible Pit of Prophaneness; that is Work enough for the first Day's Journey. 2. Through the Brook of sincere Repentance, or true Contrition, (for every one that leaves open Prophaneness is not truly penitent). 3. Down the Valley of Self-denial, a very difficult Passage. 4. Over the Mountains of Opposition, for the Devil and all will straitway make head against him. 5. Over the Stile of carnal Reason. . . . 6. In to the pleasant Ways of the New Covenant. 7. So upon the Top of the Rock of Ages, and there he may take a Prospect of his own Country.

Seventeenth-century writers described the steps and hurdles differently but clung to the basic metaphor.

top of Mount Pisgah, thence taking a clear prospect of the Land of promise . . . ?" [10]

But after Crusoe's prospect he still has "some rough Way to pass yet" (B89), and soon he and his companions discover that, like the ancient Hebrews, they have to fight their way into their promised land. Their enemies are ravenous wolves, and the innocent company (all making their first journey through this hostile territory) does not know how to cope with such organized ferocity. Crusoe, however, although inexperienced with this specific kind of danger, demonstrates his mastery, for seeing a hundred wolves "coming on directly towards us . . . as regularly as an Army" (B97), he senses what to do, and, like Joshua, achieves his purpose by making great noises with the few weapons he had and by having the company unite in a great shout.[11] A second, even greater battle follows as night comes on and some three hundred wolves gather for the attack, but again Crusoe's strategy delivers the company. The noise of the "hellish Creatures" increases as the company approaches "the Entrance of a Wood, through which we were to pass, at the farther side of the Plain" (B98),[12] and the carcasses of two horses and two partially eaten men suddenly appear. Several volleys of shot deter the wolves temporarily, but soon the charge is renewed. At last, Crusoe contrives a trick derived from another biblical metaphor: he builds a wall of fire between the men and wolves,[13] then leads the company in a final shout which subdues the enemy. The hero of this episode is clearly a far different Crusoe from the fear-ridden young man who, unable even to follow orders,

[10] (London, 1700), p. 166.

[11] See Josh. 6.

[12] Here the language is very like that of Bunyan.

[13] Zech. 2:5 describes God as a "wall of fire," protecting his chosen. In comparing the world to a wilderness Benjamin Keach says this: "In a howling Wilderness a Wall of Fire is exceeding necessary to preserve from Wild and ravenous beasts: God upon this account is said to be a Wall of Fire to his People, whilst they remain in this World, amongst the Sons of *Belial* . . ." (*Tropologia*, II, 392). John Flavell argues that this biblical metaphor derives from such an "ancient custom of travellers in the desarts" (*Navigation Spiritualized; or a New Compass for Seamen* [Newburyport, 1796; first published, 1664], p. 72).

faints at the pump during an early voyage[14] and who runs about his island, when he first arrives there, wringing his hands distractedly.

The episode of the wolves, like the final dramatic episodes in pilgrim literature, demonstrates that man is not really "delivered" until he is safe at his final destination, a point contemporary theologians stressed tirelessly. "Be not discouraged," writes John Flavell in his *Mount Pisgah* (1689), "if you should meet with some difficulties, even on the borders of the Land of Promise." [15] *"The Israelites,"* adds George Swinnock in *The Christian-Mans Calling* (Volume II, 1663), *"could not enjoy the land flowing with milk and hony, till they had fought with, and conquered the Cananites, and forced their way through grievous obstacles and oppositions."* [16] Crusoe considers his struggle with wolves the most difficult battle he has fought. "I was never so sensible of Danger in my life," Crusoe reports, ". . . and . . . I gave my self over for lost . . ." (B102).

Ultimately, Crusoe's battle here suggests one of the novel's major concerns, the war between good and evil. Crusoe's final victory over bestiality culminates a pattern which had begun early in his life with encounters against a lion, a leopard, and a nameless beast on the coast of Africa, and which had recently included a comic encounter with a bear.[17] The beasts subdued by Crusoe are standard biblical symbols of evil, forces which God's elect (lambs) must overcome during their pilgrimage. John Flavell suggests the typical Puritan use of the bestial metaphor in these doggerel lines from *Navigation Spiritualized* (1664):

> This world's a forest, where from day to day,
> Bears, wolves, and lions range and seek their prey,
> Amidst them all poor harmless Lambs are fed,
> And by their very dens in safety led.

[14] When Crusoe faints, his companions show little respect. "No body minded me," reports Crusoe, "or what was become of me; but another Man stept up to the Pump, and thrusting me aside with his Foot, let me lye . . ." (A12).

[15] P. 42.

[16] Fol. B2^{v}.

[17] Friday becomes a comic figure in this scene, perhaps to emphasize his parallel with the novel's other comic figure, Xury. Crusoe's conduct relative to the two servants dramatizes the difference in his attitudes and conduct before and after conversion.

. . . .
He that to raging seas such bonds hath put
The mouths of ravenous beasts can also shut.
. . . .
Shun sin, keep close to Christ; for other Evils
You need not fear, tho compast round with devils.[18]

The young Crusoe misses the significance of his early encounters, but by the end of his journey he comprehends his battle in larger terms. The wolves, Crusoe reports (and he later repeats the simile), "came on like Devils . . ." (B100).

When the company is safely delivered across the mountains, men who have previously made the same journey tell Crusoe and his friends (in language suggestive of pilgrim allegory) that their experiences are "nothing but what was ordinary in the great Forest at the Foot of the Mountains" (B101), and these seasoned travelers relate better and easier ways to defeat the enemy. But Crusoe's company, happy to have negotiated the journey by any means, basks in the secure comfort of their new land, "where we found a warm Climate, a fruitful pleasant Country, and no Snow, no Wolves, or any Thing like them . . ." (B101).

Defoe is able to use the physical to reflect the spiritual quite easily in *Robinson Crusoe*, for the novel's plot follows the comprehensive metaphor which is basic to Puritan tradition and which had

[18] Pp. 91 92. The episode of the wolves also climaxes the motif of savagery which runs through the novel. Beginning with his early travels along the barbarian coast, Crusoe continually encounters the savagery of men and beasts, but by the end of the last episode he has shown himself capable of subduing bestiality in any form. Keach articulates the standard beast emblems this way: "In a Wilderness are many wild and devouring Beasts, so that 'tis dangerous to dwell in it, or pass through it: So this World abounds with cruel and unmerciful Men, who are called Wolves, Lions, Bears, Dogs, Dragons, &c. by which means God's People are always exposed to great Trouble and Danger, whilst they remain therein" (*Tropologia*, II, 391). Sometimes, as in Dante, biblical beasts such as those in Daniel 7 are made symbols of *specific* human evils, but Puritan literature usually suggested less precise symbolism for the beasts man met in the wilderness of this world.

taken a fictional form in pilgrim allegory. The journey metaphor (for man's temporary sojourn on earth) derives ultimately from the Bible, but the metaphor's wide popularity in the seventeenth and eighteenth centuries results from new Puritan modes of thinking. In the Puritan tradition, the journey most often becomes a sea voyage: man before conversion is aimlessly adrift on the wide sea and after conversion sails (against prevailing winds) toward the heavenly port. The metaphor is often extended to include life's major experiences: temptations and sins become rocks; man's uncontrollable natural propensity becomes blasts, storms, and tempests which drive him from his course; failure to overcome temptation becomes shipwreck or drowning. Sermons and guide books repeat the metaphor frequently, but the most sustained use comes in pilgrim literature. Here the metaphor is fundamental to the structure; man's entire life, the subject of the pilgrim writers, is dramatized as a journey—a journey taking place in a physical world but having a spiritual import.

Like *The Pilgrim's Progress, Robinson Crusoe* is sustained by the metaphor. Pilgrim allegory and Defoe's novel are nourished by the same Puritan traditions, and they share the same theological view of the world and man's role in it. Though it devotes more attention to man's life before conversion than does most pilgrim literature, *Robinson Crusoe* presents the same story of rebellion and punishment, repentance and salvation, which is common to Puritan spiritual histories, whether in the form of providence stories, *exempla* in guide books, spiritual biographies, or pilgrim allegories. Defoe's hero, unlike Bunyan's, or even Richardson's, does not begin with the single-minded determination and the almost supernatural power to overcome satanic adversaries. What aims he has are negative— determination not to follow the approved course—but after drifting over tempestuous seas, being cast upon shores half a world apart, and coming close to perishing upon treacherous, unseen rocks, he learns an important lesson. In utter distress, desolation, and loneliness, Crusoe finds in God's grace the power to overcome a hostile world of hunger and sickness, animal and human brutality, even the power to overcome his most dangerous adversary, himself. An Everyman, Crusoe begins as a wanderer, aimless on a sea he does not understand; he ends as a pilgrim, crossing a final mountain to enter the promised land.

Moll Flanders

by Ian Watt

I

Here is an episode from the later life of Moll Flanders as a thief:

> The next thing of moment was an attempt at a gentlewoman's
> gold watch. It happened in a crowd, at a meeting house, where I was
> in very great danger of being taken. I had full hold of her watch, but
> giving a great jostle as if somebody had thrust me against her, and in
> the juncture giving the watch a fair pull, I found it would not come,
> so I let it go that moment, and cried as if I had been killed, that
> somebody had trod upon my foot, and that there was certainly
> pickpockets there, for somebody or other had given a pull at my
> watch; for you are to observe that on these adventures we always
> went very well dressed, and I had very good clothes on, and a gold
> watch by my side, as like a lady as other folks.
>
> I had no sooner said so but the other gentlewoman cried out, "A
> Pickpocket," too, for somebody, she said, had tried to pull her watch
> away.
>
> When I touched her watch I was close to her, but when I cried out
> I stopped as it were short, and the crowd bearing her forward a little,
> she made a noise too, but it was at some distance from me, so that
> she did not in the least suspect me; but when she cried out, "A
> Pickpocket," somebody cried out, "Ay, and here has been another;
> this gentlewoman has been attempted too."
>
> At that very instant, a little farther in the crowd, and very luckily

"Moll Flanders." From "Defoe as Novelist: Moll Flanders" in *The Rise of the
Novel: Studies in Defoe, Richardson and Fielding*, by Ian Watt, pp. 96–101, 104–6,
108–15. Originally published in 1957 by the University of California Press;
reprinted by permission of The Regents of the University of California and Chatto
and Windus Ltd., London.

too, they cried out, "A Pickpocket," again, and really seized a young fellow in the very fact. This, though unhappy for the wretch, was very opportunely for my case, though I had carried it handsomely enough before; but now it was out of doubt, and all the loose part of the crowd ran that way, and the poor boy was delivered up to the rage of the street, which is a cruelty I need not describe, and which however, they are always glad of, rather than be sent to Newgate, where they lie often a long time and sometimes they are hanged, and the best they can look for, if they are convicted is to be transported.[1]

It is very convincing. The gold watch is a real object, and it won't come, even with "a fair pull." The crowd is composed of solid bodies, pushing forwards and backwards, and lynching another pickpocket in the street outside. All this happens in a real, particular place. It is true that, as is his custom, Defoe makes no attempt to describe it in detail, but the little glimpses that emerge win us over completely to its reality. A dissenting meeting-house is a piquant choice for these activities, to be sure, but Defoe does not arouse suspicion that he is a literary man by drawing attention to its ironic inappropriateness.

If we have any doubts, they are concerned, not with the authenticity of the episode, but with its literary status. The vividness of the scene itself is curiously incidental. Defoe gets into the middle of the action, with "I had full hold of her watch," and then suddenly changes from laconic reminiscent summary to a more detailed and immediate presentation, as though only to back up the truth of his initial statement. Nor has the scene been planned as a coherent whole: we are soon interrupted in the middle of the scene by an aside explaining something that might have been explained before, the important fact that Moll Flanders was dressed like a gentlewoman herself: this transition adds to our trust that no ghost-writer has been imposing order on Moll Flanders's somewhat rambling reminiscences, but if we had seen Moll dressed "as like a lady as other folks" from the beginning, the action would have run more strongly, because uninterruptedly, into the next incident of the scene—the raising of the alarm.

[1] *Moll Flanders*, ed. Aitken (London, 1902), II, 19–20.

Defoe goes on to stress the practical moral, which is that the gentlewoman should have "seized the next body that was behind her," instead of crying out. In so doing, Defoe lives up to the didactic purpose professed in the "Author's Preface," but at the same time he directs our attention to the important problem of what the point of view of the narrator is supposed to be. We presume that it is a repentant Moll, speaking towards the end of her life: it is therefore surprising that in the next paragraph she should gaily describe her "governess's" procuring activities as "pranks." Then a further confusion about the point of view becomes apparent: we notice that to Moll Flanders other pickpockets, and the criminal fraternity in general, are a "they," not a "we." She speaks as though she were not implicated in the common lot of criminals; or is it, perhaps, Defoe who has unconsciously dropped into the "they" he himself would naturally use for them? And earlier, when we are told that "the other gentlewoman" cried out, we wonder why the word "other"? Is Moll Flanders being ironical about the fact that she too was dressed like a gentlewoman, or has Defoe forgotten that, actually, she is not?

Nor are these doubts about the completeness of Defoe's control over his narrative dispelled by the relationship, or rather lack of relationship, between this passage and the rest of the book. The transition to the next episode is somewhat confusing. It is effected, first by the address to the reader explaining how to deal with pickpockets, and then by a somewhat confusing *résumé* of the governess's life which is introduced by the words: "I had another adventure, which puts this matter out of doubt, and which may be an instruction for posterity in the case of a pickpocket." We and posterity, however, remain uninstructed, since the ensuing adventure turns out to be concerned with shoplifting: it seems likely that Defoe did not have the end of his paragraph in mind when he began it, and improvised an expository transition to mark time until some other incident suggested itself.

The connection between the meeting-house scene and the narrative as a whole confirms the impression that Defoe paid little attention to the internal consistency of his story. When she is transported to Virginia Moll Flanders gives her son a gold watch as a memento of their reunion; she relates how she "desired he would now and then kiss it for my sake," and then adds sardonically that she did not tell him "that I stole it from a gentlewoman's side, at a meeting house in London." [2] Since there is no other episode in *Moll Flanders* dealing with watches, gentlewomen and meeting-houses, we must surely infer that Defoe had a faint recollection of what he had written a hundred pages earlier about the attempt on the gentlewoman's gold watch, but forgot that it had failed.

These discontinuities strongly suggest that Defoe did not plan his novel as a coherent whole, but worked piecemeal, very rapidly, and without any subsequent revision. This is indeed very likely on other grounds. His main aim as a writer was certainly to achieve a large and effective output—over fifteen hundred pages of print in the year that saw *Moll Flanders*; and this output was not primarily intended for a careful and critical audience. That Defoe had very little of the author's usual fastidious attitude to his work, or even of the author's sensitiveness to adverse criticism, is very evident from the terms of his prefatory apology for the poetic imperfections of the work of which he was perhaps most proud, *The True-Born Englishman*: ". . . without being taken for a conjuror, I may venture to foretell, that I shall be cavilled at about my mean style, rough verse, and incorrect language, things I indeed might have taken more care in. But the book is printed; and though I see some faults, it is too late to mend them. And this is all I think needful to say. . . ." If Defoe was as nonchalant as this about an early work, and a poem at that, it is surely unlikely that he gave a second thought to the possible inconsistencies in a work of popular fiction such as *Moll Flanders*; especially as, for such an ill-regarded and ephemeral kind of writing, his publisher would probably not have offered the extra payment which Defoe would apparently have required for revising his manuscript.

[2] Aitken, II, 158.

Defoe's very casual attitude to his writing goes far to explain the inconsistencies in matters of detail which are very common in all his works; the same lack of coherent initial plan or of later revision can be surmised in the nature of his narrative method.

Nearly all novels employ a combination of two different methods of reporting: relatively full scenic presentation where, at a definite time and place, the doings of the characters are reported more or less fully; and passages of barer and less detailed summary which set the stage and provide a necessary connective framework. The tendency of most novelists is to reduce these latter synopses to a minimum and to focus as much attention as possible on a few fully realised scenes; but this is not the case with Defoe. His story is told in over a hundred realised scenes whose average length is less than two pages, and an equally large number of passages containing rapid and often perfunctory connective synopses.

The effect is obvious: almost every page offers evidence of the fall in tension as we switch from episode to summary—for a minute Moll Flanders will appear brilliantly illumined, only to fall back into the semi-darkness of confused recollection. It is certain that it is the fully presented episodes which include all that is vivid and memorable in *Moll Flanders*, and which are rightly quoted by enthusiasts as evidence of Defoe's narrative genius; but they surely forget how large a proportion of the book is occupied by uninspired summary, plaster over an inordinate number of cracks. Defoe, certainly, makes no effort to reduce the amount of patchwork required by consolidating the episodes into as large units as possible. The first main group of episodes, for example, when Moll is seduced by the Elder Brother, is divided into a very large number of separate encounters between the characters concerned, each of whose effectiveness is largely dissipated as the narrative relapses into bare summary. Similarly Moll's reaction to the discovery of the incestuous nature of her marriage to her half-brother is split up into so many separate scenes that the emotional force of the episode as a whole is much weakened.

This somewhat primitive aspect of Defoe's narrative technique is partly a reflection of the nature of his basic literary purpose—to produce a convincing likeness to the autobiographical memoir of a real person; and it will therefore require further examination in this larger context. First, however, the present analysis of the meeting-house passage must be concluded by a brief consideration of what is surely its most strikingly successful aspect—its prose.

Defoe's prose is not in the ordinary sense well-written, but it is remarkably effective in keeping us very close to the consciousness of Moll Flanders as she struggles to make her recollection clear: as we read we feel that nothing but an exclusive concentration on this single aim could account for such complete disregard of normal stylistic considerations—the repetitons and parentheses, the unpremeditated and sometimes stumbling rhythm, the long and involved sequences of co-ordinate clauses. The length of the sentences might at first sight seem to interfere with the effect of spontaneous authenticity; but in fact the lack of marked pauses within the sentences, and the frequent recapitulations, tend to heighten the effect.

The most remarkable thing about the prose of the passage is perhaps the fact that it is Defoe's usual style. No previous author's normal way of writing could so credibly have passed for the characteristic utterance of such an uneducated person as Moll Flanders. . . .

II

Defoe's novels are landmarks in the history of fiction largely because they are the first considerable narratives which embody all the elements of formal realism. But although formal realism helps to define the uniqueness of the novel, it obviously does not by any means exhaust our critical disiderata about it; the novel may have a distinctive representational technique, but if it is to be considered a valuable literary form it must also have, like any other literary form, a structure which is a coherent expression of all its parts. Our preliminary examination has suggested several doubts about the coherence of *Moll Flanders*; and this, combined with the extent of the critical disagreement about Defoe's status as a novelist, makes necessary a fuller analysis of its total structure, and particularly of the relationship between three of its main components, plot, character and moral theme.

A brief recapitulation of the plot of *Moll Flanders* will make clear its episodic nature. The story falls into two main parts; the first and longer one devoted to the heroine's career as a wife, and the second to her criminal activities and their consequences. The first part is composed of five main episodes, each of them ended by the death or departure of a husband; and there are two main sub-episodes, one of them concerning the abortive affair with a married man at Bath, and the other with the stratagems whereby her friend the Redriff widow secures a mate.

It is true that three of the main episodes are not wholly independent. The first marriage, closely related as it is both with Moll's first efforts to improve her condition and her seduction by the Elder Brother, forms a satisfactory and indeed symbolic prelude to the novel as a whole, although it has no later connection with the plot. The third marriage, with her half-brother, leads to the discovery of the secret of her birth, and thus has links both with the beginning of Moll's life and with the final scenes in Virginia where she finds him and her son again. While the fourth marriage, to James or Jemmy, the Irish, Lancashire or highwayman husband (it is typical of Defoe's onomastic nonchalance that such copious alternative identifications should seem desirable), is connected to the later part of the book from Moll's trial at the Old Bailey onwards. On the other hand, although some of the plot components in the first part are related to each other, the interlocking remains rudimentary, and during long intervals it is wholly submerged in the details of Moll's other activities.

The second, and for many readers the most interesting, part of the book is mainly devoted to Moll's career as a thief; its only connection with the rest of the plot is that it finally leads first to her arrest, then to the reunion with James in prison, to her later transportation, and eventually to her return to Virginia and her family there. Ultimately, therefore, Moll's criminal adventures end in a renewal of our contact with the two main episodes of the earlier half of the plot, and thus make possible a fairly neat conclusion to the novel as a whole.

This degree of continuity, based on the relationships between the heroine, her mother, half-brother, favourite husband and only significant child, gives *Moll Flanders* a degree of structural coherence which makes it unique among Defoe's novels. The only comparable plot is that of *Roxana*, and there the unifying mechanism, though simpler, is somewhat similar: a child grown to maturity, relic of the seamy past, haunts the present and the heroine's possibilities of prosperous retirement. In neither novel, however, does Defoe show any clear intention of winding up his plot with any sense of completeness or finality. In *Roxana*, after taking the mother-daughter relationship with a seriousness which seems to be tending to a tragic *dénouement,* he ends the novel with the whole matter in the air; while *Moll Flanders* closes in some confusion with the heroine and later her husband coming back to England. Even when a resolution of the plot would seem to be both easy and logical, Defoe apparently prefers and certainly achieves the inconsequential and the incomplete.

These inconclusive endings are typical of Defoe, and in one sense they are undeniably effective; they serve as a final reminder that the order of the narrative is determined only by the sequence of actual events in the lives of the protagonists. Defoe flouts the orderliness of literature to demonstrate his total devotion to the disorderliness of life. . . .

Moll Flanders is certainly, as E. M. Forster says, a novel of character;[3] the plot throws the whole burden of interest on the heroine, and many readers have felt that she supports it trium-

---

[3] *Aspects of the Novel* (London, 1927), p. 61.

phantly. On the other hand, Leslie Stephen has reproached Defoe
with a lack of "all that goes by the name of psychological analysis in
modern fiction," [4] and not altogether without justification, at least if
our emphasis is on the word analysis. There is probably no episode
in *Moll Flanders* where the motivation is unconvincing, but for
somewhat damaging reasons—few of the situations confronting
Defoe's heroine call for any more complex discriminations than
those of Pavlov's dog: Defoe makes us admire the speed and
resolution of Moll's reactions to profit or danger; and if there are no
detailed psychological analyses, it is because they would be wholly
superfluous.

There are two main ways in which later novelists have mani-
fested their powers of psychological understanding: indirectly, by
revealing the character's personality through his actions; or directly, by specific analysis of the character's various states of mind.
Both these methods, of course, can be and usually are combined;
and they are usually found in conjunction with a narrative
structure designed to embody the character's development, and to
present him with crucial moral choices which bring his whole
personality into play. There is very little of these things in *Moll
Flanders*. Defoe does not so much portray his heroine's character as
assume its reality in every action, and carry his reader with him—if
we accede to the reality of the deed, it is difficult to challenge the
reality of the doer. It is only when we attempt to fit all her acts
together, and see them as an expression of a single personality, that
doubts arise; nor are these doubts allayed when we discover how
little we are told about some of the things we should need to know
for a full picture of her personality, and how some of the things we
are told seem contradictory.

These deficiencies are especially apparent in Defoe's treatment of
personal relationships. We are told very little, for example, about
the quality of Moll Flanders's loves, and even our information
about their quantity is suspiciously meagre. When she accuses

---

[4] "Defoe's Novels," *Hours in a Library* (London, 1899), I, 17.

herself of having "lain with thirteen men," we cannot but resent the fact that some six lovers have been hidden not only from her fifth husband, but, much more unforgiveably, from us. Even among those lovers we know, we cannot be sure which Moll preferred. We have a strong impression that James is her favourite, and that she leaves him for the fifth or banking one only out of dire economic necessity; yet she tells us that on her honeymoon with the latter she "never lived four pleasanter days together," and that five years of an "uninterrupted course of ease and content" ensued. When James later reappears, however, our earlier impression recurs with renewed force:

> He turned pale, and stood speechless, like one thunderstruck, and, not able to conquer the surprise, said no more but this, "Let me sit down"; and sitting down by a table, he laid his elbow on the table, and leaning his head on his hand, fixed his eyes on the ground as one stupid. I cried so vehemently, on the other hand, that it was a good while ere I could speak any more; but after I had given some vent to my passion by tears, I repeated the same words, "My dear, do you not know me?" At which he answered, Yes, and said no more a good while.[5]

Defoe's laconic narrative manner could be supremely evocative when it was focussed on personal relationships, but this happened rather rarely, probably because neither Defoe nor Moll Flanders conceived of such intangible concerns as important and continuing elements in human life. We are certainly given very little help in understanding Moll's conflicting feelings during her marriage with the banker. Like the first two husbands, he is individualised only to the extent of being given an ordinal number; and Moll's life with him is treated as a brief and wholly self-contained episode whose emotional premise does not have to be reconciled with other features of her life and character. Defoe, indeed, emphasises this discontinuity by telling us that James wrote three times to Moll at this time suggesting that they go off to Virginia as she had earlier

[5] *Hours*, I, 190, 196, 197; II, 113–114.

proposed,[6] but only after the fifth husband has been long dead: another novelist would have made such pleas an opportunity for clarifying his heroine's conflicting feelings towards the two men, but Defoe gives us only the bare facts, long after they have lost their potential power for psychological illumination.

If we attempt to draw any conclusion from Defoe's treatment of these particular personal relationships it must surely be that Moll Flanders was unaffectedly happy with both husbands, and that although her love of one of them was deeper, she did not allow this sentiment to interfere with the solid comforts which the other was able to provide. She is, obviously, affectionate but no sentimentalist. We get a somewhat different picture, however, when we come to consider her character, not as a wife, but as a mother. On the one hand, she can behave with complete sentimental abandon, as when she kisses the ground her long-separated son Humphrey has been standing on; on the other hand, although she shows some fondness for two or three of her children, she is by normal standards somewhat callous in her treatment of most of them—the majority are mentioned only to be forgotten, and, once left in the care of relatives or foster-mothers, are neither redeemed subsequently nor even inquired after when opportunity permits. Here the conclusion about her character must surely be that, although there are extenuating circumstances, she is often a heartless mother. It is difficult to see how this can be reconciled either with her kissing the ground that Humphrey has trodden, or with the fact that she herself loudly condemns unnatural mothers,[7] but never makes any such accusation against herself even in her deepest moments of penitent self-reprobation.

One explanation of this apparent contradiction would make it a matter, not of psychological understanding but of literary technique: briefly that in reading Defoe we must posit a kind of limited liability for the narrative, accepting whatever is specifically stated,

[6] *Hours*, II, 117.
[7] *Hours*, I, 180–183.

but drawing no inferences from omissions, however significant they may seem. If Moll Flanders does not seem to regret James during her fifth marital career, this is only because Defoe did not conceive of the attitudes of characters to each other as enduring realities on which his narrative technique should focus. If Moll Flanders is silent about the eventual fate of all her children except Humphrey and the four reported dead, we must not infer that she is without proper maternal feeling, but only that Defoe did not keep his characters in mind when they were off the stage. In both cases, in fact, our interpretation should not be allowed to go beyond what is positively stated by Defoe or Moll Flanders.

There is also another explanation for the lack of full evidence from which to deduce Moll Flanders's personality through her conduct of personal relations: the fact that the criminal individualism which Moll pursues in her later days tends to minimise the importance of personal relationships. Like the other inhabitants of the criminal milieu, she has to assume false names and false identities, and much of her life is devoted to maintaining these pretences. Nearly all her personal contacts, therefore, are coloured by this role; they can never be deep or unreserved, and they are necessarily transitory in a sense, therefore Defoe is being realistic when he portrays the personal relationships of Moll Flanders as a series of essentially casual encounters, very like those of the real vagrants and criminals described by Mayhew in the next century. Here is one such report:

> In the morning I was turned out [from a union], and after I had left I picked up with a young woman who had slept in the union overnight. I said I was going on the road across country to Birmingham, and I axed her to go with me. I had never seen her before. She consented and we went along together begging our way. . . . I lost the young woman when I was put in prison in Manchester. She never came to see me in quod. She cared nothing for me. She only kept company with me to have someone on the road along with her; and I didn't care for her, not I.[8]

[8] *Mayhew's Characters*, ed. Quennell (London, 1951), pp. 294–296.

The laconic authenticity of this passage is very similar to that of Defoe, and it typifies the desultory nature of personal relations in the criminal milieu. This milieu, indeed, has effects on personal relations not unlike those which economic individualism produces in *Robinson Crusoe*; Mayhew's vagrant, Moll Flanders, and most of Defoe's other characters all belong on Crusoe's island; essentially solitary, they take a severely functional view of their fellows.

Neither Defoe's narrative focus, then, nor the nature of his subject, is such as to reveal Moll's personality through the part she plays in personal relationships. This does not in itself undermine the plausibility of Defoe's presentation of his heroine's psychology: some of the apparent discrepancies noted above are mainly negative—the result of lack of information: while the basic difficulty might reasonably be resolved by assuming that Moll Flanders is naturally warm-hearted but that circumstances often force her to play a lone hand. The very fact that Moll Flanders has no stable setting in personal relationships, however, presents considerable difficulties in determining whether this is so. Usually when we attempt to make up our minds about anyone's total personality we take into account as many views about the person as possible, and by comparing them with our own are able to achieve a kind of stereoscopic effect.

No such enlightenment is forthcoming on Defoe's heroine. The episodic nature of the plot means that, although there are some two hundred characters in *Moll Flanders*, no one of them knows the heroine for more than a fraction of her career; while the autobiographical mode of presentation means that their attitudes to Moll Flanders are only given to us if and how she wishes. Their evidence actually reveals a unanimity of a very suspect kind—Defoe's heroine apparently excites in those best qualified to judge her— James, the Governess, Humphry, for instance—the most unqualified and selfless devotion. On the other hand, the reader, observing that Moll Flanders herself is never wholly honest and disinterested in her dealings with them, or indeed with anyone else, may well feel inclined to interpret their apparent adoration as evidence of a paranoid delusion on Moll Flanders's part rather than as an accurate appraisal of her character on theirs. Everyone seems to exist only for her, and no one seems to resent it. One might have expected the Governess, for example, to regret Moll's reformation since it deprives her of a prize source of stolen goods; instead, she becomes "a true penitent" [9] as soon as the heroine has no further use for her services.

If none of those close to Moll Flanders seem at all aware of her true character, and if we continue to suspect that her own account of herself may be partial, our only remaining resource for an objective view of her personality is Defoe himself. Here again, however, we at once encounter difficulties. For Moll Flanders is suspiciously like her author, even in matters where we would expect striking and obvious differences. The facts show that she is a woman and a criminal, for example; but neither of these roles determines her personality as Defoe has drawn it.

Moll Flanders, of course, has many feminine traits; she has a keen eye for fine clothes and clean linen, and shows a wifely concern for the creature comforts of her males. Further, the early pages of the book undoubtedly present a young girl with a lifelike clarity, and later there are many touches of a rough cockney humour that is undeniably feminine in tone. But these are relatively external and minor matters, and the essence of her character and actions is, to one reader at least, essentially masculine. This is a personal impression, and would be difficult, if not impossible, to establish: but it is at least certain that Moll accepts none of the disabilities of her sex, and indeed one cannot but feel that Virginia Woolf's admiration for her was largely due to admiration of a heroine who so fully realised one of the ideals of feminism: freedom from any involuntary involvement in the feminine role.

Moll Flanders is also similar to her author in another respect: she seems fundamentally untouched by her criminal background, and,

[9] *Hours*, II, 102.

on the contrary, displays many of the attitudes of a virtuous and public-minded citizen. Here, again, there is no glaring inconsistency, but there is a marked pattern of attitudes which distinguishes Moll from other members of her class: in the passage quoted above she showed no fellow-feeling for the boy pickpocket; later she is full of virtuous indignation at the "hardened wretches" of Newgate, and they repay in kind by hooting at her derisively; and when finally she is transported she has the satisfaction of observing, from her privileged comfort in the captain's quarters, that the "old fraternity" are "kept under hatches." [10] Moll Flanders obviously places criminals into two classes: most of them are vicious reprobates who richly deserve their fate; but she and a few of her friends are essentially virtuous and deserving people who have been unfortunate—she is even morally pure in her whoring since it is, as she assures us, by necessity and not "for the sake of the vice." [11] Like Defoe, in fact, she is a good Puritan who, despite a few necessary and regrettable compromises, has, in the main and in defiance of illustrious precedent, lived in a world of pitch and not been defiled.

It is this freedom from the probable psychological and social consequences of everything she does which is the central implausibility of her character as Defoe has drawn it. It applies, not only to her crimes, but to everything she does. If we take the incest theme, for example, we find that although her half-brother becomes incapable in body and mind mainly because Moll Flanders has left him, after revealing her terrible secret, she herself is quite unaffected by the circumstance, once she has left Virginia. Nor are her son's feelings towards her influenced, apparently, by the fact that he is the offspring of an incestuous marriage; nor even by the fact that his mother, after deserting him for some twenty years, only returns because, having been transported back to his vicinity, she thinks that she may now have an estate to inherit, an estate which he would otherwise enjoy.

[10] *Hours*, II, 90, 112, 90; I, 62–63; II, 134.
[11] *Hours*, I, 131, 139.

Moll Flanders's character, then, is not noticeably affected either by her sex, by her criminal pursuits, or indeed by any of the objective factors which might have been expected to set her apart from her author; on the other hand, she shares with Defoe and most of his heroes many of the character traits that are usually regarded as middle-class. She is obsessed with gentility and keeping up appearances; her pride is much involved in knowing how to get good service and proper accommodation; and she is in her heart a rentier, for whom life has no greater terror than when her "main stock wastes apace." [12] More specifically it is apparent that, like Robinson Crusoe, she has, by some process of osmosis, picked up the vocabulary and attitudes of a tradesman. Indeed her most positive qualities are the same as Crusoe's, a restless, amoral and strenuous individualism. It is, no doubt, possible to argue that these qualities might be found in a character of her sex, station and personal vicissitudes; but it is not likely, and it is surely more reasonable to assume that all these contradictions are the consequence of a process to which first-person narration is peculiarly prone; that Defoe's identification with Moll Flanders was so complete that, despite a few feminine traits, he created a personality that was in essence his own.

[12] *Hours*, I, 131.

Moll Flanders

by Mark Schorer

Everything about *Moll Flanders*—its kind and Defoe's extension of that kind, its literary method, its paradoxical morality—everything about it has a naïvely direct relation to his own world of experience and interests. The kind is the biography of a rogue, a conventional if low form of literary expression since Elizabethan times. Rogue biographies were usually the lives of real criminals fictionally foreshortened and sensationalized. Their ostensible purpose was to expose the operations of criminals and thereby to warn; their actual purpose was rather to thrill an undiscriminating audience with melodrama. The convention offered Defoe solid elements to which he would almost at once have responded. The world of crime he had experienced and observed with sufficient directness and even fascination to recognize as a subject matter that he was in a superb position to handle, and it is no accident that Moll's paralyzing fear of Newgate is her most forcibly urged emotion. At the same time, the journalist in Defoe would have responded to a subject that lent itself to exposure, and the Puritan, to the elements that allowed the expression of a ready impulse to admonish and exhort. Add to these the convention of the "secret history," which would be as attractive to the intriguing familiar of party ministers as it would be to the journalistic spy, and the several elements that the rogue biography offered to the special talents of Daniel Defoe should be evident.

The method that Defoe developed to animate the *genre* is

perfectly calculated to his talents. The Puritan and the journalist together, the first out of genuine suspicions of the idle and the second out of his conviction that nothing is more persuasive than fact, lead Defoe to deny that he is writing fiction at all. On the contrary, he tells us, he is merely editing the diary of a real and notorious character who must, for reputation's sake, present herself under a pseudonym. Thus at once Defoe saves his conscience and puts himself into his favorite position, the assumed role. He is not telling us about Moll Flanders, he *is* Moll Flanders. The device comes easy to one whose own life had consisted of a series of conflicting roles, and he had had long practice not only in life but in his previous writings. He had written in the past as though he were a Turk, a Scotch soldier, a visionary Scotchman, a Quaker, a lonely but enterprising castaway. Why not now as a sexually abandoned thief? Once the role was assumed, it was easy, too, for the journalist to support the role, or, at any rate, for a journalist with Defoe's special feeling for the telling physical facts in any situation. Out of this gift grows his special kind of verisimilitude, that kind of realism best described as "circumstantial." It is a method that depends not on sensibility but on fact, not on description but on proof, as if a man, wishing to tell us of an excellent dinner, did not bother to say how his food tasted, but merely listed the courses that made up the meal, or, more likely, produced a cancelled check to prove that he had paid a good deal for it. On such evidence, we would hardly doubt that he had eaten it. Thus the centrality in Defoe's method (and the resulting texture) of the bolts of goods, the inventories, the itemized accounts, the landlady's bills, the lists, the ledgers.

Defoe's tone is hardly less important to this method than his persuasive details. How matter-of-fact all this is, for such an extraordinary life! Five marriages, a score of recorded lovers, and, if we can count, a score of children, twelve dead and eight alive when Moll's child-bearing ceased at last. *We* exclaim (we may even protest), but Defoe does not. In this story, the birth of a child or the acquisition of a new lover seems hardly as important as the hiring of a coach or the packing of a trunk. Defoe's prevailingly matter-of-fact tone levels all incidents out on a straight narrative plane, and we are lulled into supposing that any account of a life that is so guilelessly without emphasis is necessarily true. Defoe's deepest guile, indeed, always lay in his appearance of being without guile. A narrator with an air of uncomprehending innocence or a narrator so innocent that he comprehends precisely the wrong things in a situation, had been among Defoe's great propagandistic devices throughout his career as a journalist, and over and over again, this device had been the basis of his satire. In *Moll Flanders*, the heroine, like Defoe's earlier narrators, is peculiarly innocent; the meaning of her experience seems to run off her moral skin like quicksilver; nothing touches her; at the end, a woman of seventy, she is almost exactly as bland as she was in the opening scenes, a small girl who wished to be a lady. And this quality again, this very imperceptiveness, lends itself to Defoe's purposes of persuasion. Isn't this, we ask ourselves, exactly what a woman like Moll would be, so wonderfully imperceptive that this is really a book about a remarkable self-deception?

But then the other question comes, and with it, the question whether this is a method adequate to the production of a novel. Whose deception is it—Moll's? or Defoe's? And this question takes us into the third consideration, the paradoxical morality of the book. *Moll Flanders* comes to us professing that its purpose is to warn us not only against a life of crime but against the cost of crime. We cannot for very many pages take that profession seriously, for it is apparent all too soon that nothing in the conduct of the narrative indicates that virtue is either more necessary or more enjoyable than vice. At the end we discover that Moll turns virtuous only after a life of vice has enabled her to do so with security. The actualities of the book, then, enforce the moral assumption of any commercial culture, the belief that virtue and worldly goods form an equation. This is a morality somewhat less than skin deep, with no relation to motives arising from more than a legalistic sense of good and evil; having its relation, rather, to motives arising from the presence or absence of food, drink, linen, damask, silver, and timepieces. It is the morality of measurement, and without in the least intending it, *Moll Flanders* is our classic revelation of the mercantile mind: the morality of measurement which Defoe has apparently neglected to measure.

Defoe's announced purpose is probably a pious humbug, and he probably meant us to read the book as a series of scandalous events. His inexhaustible pleasure in excess (twenty children, not five; twenty lovers, not fifteen; five husbands, including a brother, not three)—this element in the book continues to amuse us. The book becomes indeed a vast joke, a wonderful kind of myth of female endurance, and, like all tall tales, an absurdity. Yet it is not nearly as absurd as that other absurdity that Defoe did not intend at all, the notion that Moll could live a rich and full life of crime, and by mere repentance, emerge spotless in the end, a perfect matron. The point is, of course, that she has no moral being, and that the book has no real moral life. Everything is external. Everything can be weighed, measured, handled, paid for in gold, or expiated by a prison term. To this the whole method of the novel testifies: this is a morality of social circumstance, a morality in which only externals count since only externals show. Thus we may conclude that the real meaning of the book is to be discovered in spite of Defoe, whose point of view is, finally, indistinguishable from the point of view of Moll Flanders; and we may therefore conclude, further, that the book is not the true chronicle of a disreputable female, but the true allegory of an impoverished soul—the author's; not, indeed, an anatomy of the criminal class, but of the middle class striving for security.

Security and morality are almost identical in *Moll Flanders*, and we today are hardly in a position to scorn Defoe's observation that it is easier to be pious with a bank account than without one. Like *Robinson Crusoe*, this is a desperate story of survival, a story that tries to demonstrate the possibility of success through unremitting native wit. Security, clearly, is the end of life:

> This was evidently my case, for I was now a loose, unguided creature, and had no help, no assistance, no guide for my conduct; I

knew what I aimed at and what I wanted, but knew nothing how to pursue the end by direct means. I wanted to be placed in a settled state of living, and had I happened to meet with a sober, good husband, I should have been as faithful and true a wife to him as virtue itself could have formed. If I had been otherwise, the vice came in always at the door of necessity, not at the door of inclination; and I understood too well, by the want of it, what the value of a settled life was, to do anything to forfeit the felicity of it.

But if security is the end of life, ingenuity, clever personal enterprise, is its most admirable quality, and, certainly, the only way to security:

> I have observed that the account of his life would have made a much more pleasing history than this of mine; and, indeed, nothing in it was more strange than this part, viz. that he had carried on that desperate trade full five-and-twenty years and had never been taken, the success he had met with had been so very uncommon, and such that sometimes he had lived handsomely, and retired in one place for a year or two at a time, keeping himself and a man-servant to wait on him, and had often sat in the coffee-houses and heard the very people whom he had robbed give accounts of their being robbed, and of the places and circumstances, so that he could easily remember that it was the same.

Strip *Moll Flanders* of its bland loquacity, its comic excess, its excitement, and we have the revelation of a savage life, a life that is motivated solely by economic need, and a life that is measured at last by those creature comforts that, if we gain them, allow us one final breath in which to praise the Lord. Yet this essence is not the book as we have it, as Defoe wrote it, any more than the acquisitive impulse is the whole of middle-class value. For there is also the secondary interest of the book, which is to reveal to us the condition of women, the small choice (there was only her needle; to be sure, there *was* her needle had she preferred it; but who would ask that she should have?)—the small choice that Moll could have made between disreputable and reputable employment. The infant Moll, born in Newgate, becomes a public charge; education is an impossibility; independent work is likewise an impossibility; and as young men are by nature wolves, so the world at large is wolfish. Women, like men, are forced into the realm of trade, they offer such goods as they have for such prices as they can command.

This secondary interest suggests the softer side of Daniel Defoe, his will to create a less savage world than the world he knew. The paradox of the middle class has always been its hope to create, through its values of mere measurement, values that did not have to measure in its way. And the social pathos of *our* lives is largely to be traced to our illusion that we have done so. This is also the final pathos of Moll Flanders' life, whether Defoe was aware of it or not.

Sympathy exceeds awareness, and throughout *Moll Flanders* (this is probably the main reason that we continue to read it) we are charged by the author's sympathy. It shows as much in the gusto with which he enters Moll's life and participates in her adventures as it does in his tolerance of her errors and her deceits and self-deceits. It shows, furthermore, in a few moments of this vastly episodic narrative when genuinely novelistic values emerge, when, that is, the individual character somehow shines through the social automaton. One such moment occurs when Moll is reunited with her Lancashire husband:

> As soon as he was gone, and I had shut the door, I threw off my hood, and bursting out into tears, "My dear," says I, "do you not know me?" He turned pale, and stood speechless, like one thunder-struck, and, not able to conquer the surprise, said no more but this, "Let me sit down"; and sitting down by a table, he laid his elbow upon the table, and leaning his head on his hand, fixed his eyes on the ground as one stupid. I cried so vehemently, on the other hand, that it was a good while ere I could speak any more; but after I had given some vent to my passion by tears, I repeated the same words, "My dear, do you not know me?" At which he answered, Yes, and said no more a good while.

Such genuinely moving scenes must be observed, of course, against the long stretches of the book where the relentless narrative sense points up the totally deficient sense of plot, where the carelessness of time and causality destroys the illusion of actuality after all the pains to achieve it, where the monotonously summarizing method gives even the fine feeling for separate incident a pallor. These deficiencies all remind us that this is not, after all, the first English novel.

Yet it is very nearly the first English novel. It is the whole groundwork. Given twenty more years of literary convention and just a slightly different set of interests, Defoe would have freed himself from the tyranny of fact and the morality of circumstance and sprung into the liberties of formal fiction, where another morality must prevail. His prose has been called "the prose of democracy," and this has been the characteristic prose of the novel as we know it in English. The prose of democracy is a prose without rhetorical refinement even when it employs rhetorical display; it emerges in sentences as sinewy and emphatically plain as this: "In short, they robbed together, lay together, were taken together, and at last were hanged together." It is also a prose capable of fine, colloquial surprise:

> I made him one present, and it was all I had of value, and that was one of the gold watches, of which I mentioned above, that I had two in my chest, and this I happened to have with me, and I gave it him at his third visit. I told him I had nothing of any value to bestow but that, and I desired he would now and then kiss it for my sake. I did not indeed tell him that I had stole it from a gentlewoman's side, at a meeting-house in London. That's by the way.

Such prose projects us into the future of the novel: Jane Austen, George Eliot, Mark Twain, D. H. Lawrence, Ernest Hemingway.

Yet not entirely. "That's by the way," says Moll; and then comes the voice of Defoe, saying, too, "Yes, that's by the way." He does not, finally, *judge* his material, as a novelist must. He makes us sort out his multiple materials for him and pass our judgment. Our judgment must therefore fall on him, not on his creature, Moll. In her bland, self-deluded way, she asks us not to be harsh; and that again is the voice of Defoe, taking a breath at the end to beg posterity to be kind. As it has been.

On *Moll Flanders*

by Dorothy Van Ghent

The editorial preface to a popular modern reprint of *Moll Flanders* speaks of the book as "one of the most remarkable examples of true realism in the whole range of fiction." The statement suggests that "true realism" is specifically that kind of realism which *Moll Flanders* exhibits; by implication, other kinds—if there are other kinds—would not be "true." There can be no gainsaying the realism of *Moll Flanders*: Defoe's book describes minutely the local scene, London; it refers circumstantially to contemporary customs (although not to those of the mid-seventeenth century in which Moll supposedly had her career, but to those of the early eighteenth century when Defoe was writing); it employs "documents" (Moll's "memorandums," quoted letters, hospital bills, etc.) in order to increase the illusion of verifiable fact; and, in general, it aims at "objective," "reportorial," "photographic" representation, as if from the standpoint of an artless observer. In other words, the whole book is oriented toward what we call "facts"—specifically toward those "facts" which are events and objects that have spatial-temporal determination. But it is unfortunate that factual orientation in the novel should have come to determine the definition of realism in the novel; for "realism" inevitably implies a doctrine of the "real"; and it implies, when it is used to describe the factually oriented novel, that spatial-temporal facts are the only "real," and therefore that the factually oriented novel is closer to "reality"—a more trustworthy representation of reality—than any other kind of novel. What is suggested by the statement quoted at the beginning of this essay is not an evaluation of *Moll Flanders* as literature, but a certain popular philosophical conviction of the exclusive "reality" of material facts, a conviction that the so-defined "realistic" novel seems to flatter and support; and what is blurred over by the statement is the *hypothetical* structure of even the most "documentary" or "circumstantial" kind of fiction, a hypothetical structure that it shares generically with all fiction.

The hypothesis on which *Moll Flanders* is based might be phrased in this way: given a human creature "conditioned" to react only to material facts, then the world where that person lived might cogently assume the shape that Moll's world assumes—a shape astonishingly without spiritual dimension. In a parallel fashion one might phrase the hypothesis on which *The Pilgrim's Progress* is based: given a person for whom relationship with God was the only "reality," then, in his world, material facts would show as misleading appearances, and the shape taken by his adventures would be altogether spiritually dimensioned. If the world of the particular novel is to create itself fully for us, we must waive for the moment our own *a priori* convictions as to whether material fact or relationship with God is the prime reality; we must approach the fictional hypothesis with as much respect for its conditions and as much attention to its logic as we would give to a scientific or mathematical hypothesis. Defoe's "realism" must be looked upon as a consistent use of certain devices for the creation of a special kind of world, just as Bunyan's allegorical method is a consistent use of certain devices (some of them "realistic" in the same sense as Defoe's) for the creation of a special kind of world. Eventually, the trained and sensitized reader finds that novels called "realistic" are as symbolic as Bunyan's allegory.

The questions we must ask of *Moll Flanders* are those we ask of any other novel: what are its elements? how are they made to cohere in a unity? how are its special technical devices (in this case, those of "realism") appropriate to the making of this particular world? We notice, for instance, that Moll's world contains many *things* — tangible things such as watches and wigs and yardage goods and necklaces and dresses and barrels and bales and bottles and trunks. We may make some judgment as to the kind of world presented in a novel simply on the basis of the frequency with which an author uses certain substantives and images, to the exclusion of others. In *Moll*, there is relatively great frequency in the use of words naming that kind of object which constitutes material wealth. This singularity of *Moll Flanders* becomes striking when we try to remember how many dresses Christiana had for her long journey, and whether Mr. Worldly Wiseman wore a wig or carried a watch.

But let us make a further distinction: these tangible, material objects with which Moll is so deeply concerned are not at all vivid in texture. When Moll tells us that she put on a "good pearl necklace," we do not know whether the pearls were large or small or graded or uniform in size, or whether the necklace hung low on her bosom or was wound around her throat three times, nor do we know if the pearls were real or artificial; the word "good" here indicates simply that the pearls looked costly to a sophisticated eye, and were of a kind that a woman of substantial social position might wear; the "good pearl necklace" is mentioned not in a way that will make a sense image for us, but only in a way that will suggest the market value of the necklace and (through the market value) its value as an indicator of social prestige. Similarly, when she tells us that she gave her son a fine gold watch, we have no sense image of the watch; we do not know its size or design or delicacy or heft; we know only that it is a watch which would bring a good price. Therefore, in saying that the world of *Moll Flanders* is made up to a large extent of *things,* we do not mean that it is a world rich in physical, sensuous textures—in images for the eye or for the tactile sense or for the tongue or the ear or for the sense of temperature or the sense of pressure. It is extraordinarily barren of such images. And yet sense images are certainly "real" even in a

world exclusively composed of "facts"; they are the constant means
by which we are made aware of facts (the scientific observer himself
is dependent upon their evidence). Clearly, then, an intense
selectivity has limited the facts of Moll Flanders' world to a certain
few kinds of facts, and has ignored great masses of other facts that
we think of as making up the plenum of factual reality. Such
selectivity warns us that this realistic novel is not actually an
"objective," "reportorial," "photographic" representation of reality; its selectivity is that of the work of art, whose purpose is not that
of an "objective" report.

What is important in Moll's world of things is the counting,
measuring, pricing, weighing, and evaluating of the things in terms
of the wealth they represent and the social status they imply for the
possessor. What is unimportant (and we learn as much by what is
unimportant as by what is important) is sensuous life, the concrete
experience of things as they have individual texture. The unimpor-
tance of sensuous life in Moll's world is fairly astonishing inasmuch
as Moll herself is a lusty, full-bodied, lively-sensed creature. Our
instrument or medium of knowledge about Moll's world is Moll.
The medium is a sensual medium (what woman, weak in sensuality, would remark, as Moll does: "I never was in bed with my
husband, but I wished myself in the arms of his brother . . . in
short, I committed adultery and incest with him every day in my
desires . . ." or would have given us the scenes in the inns at
Gloucester and Bath?); but communicated through this medium is
an assemblage of objects entirely desensualized, inaccessible to
sense, abstract—abstract because represented only by name and by
market value on the commercial and social markets. We may speak
of this contradiction as an irony, and we shall wish to use the word
"irony" here as indicating one characteristic *mode of relationship
between elements in a novelistic structure.* Irony can imply many kinds of
discrepancy, contrast, contradiction; paradox is a form of irony;
there is irony in a statement that appears to say one thing and
actually signifies another; and there is irony in a life situation or in
a story situation that contrasts with or contradicts what might be

expected from certain of the circumstances. We are always aware of Moll's sensuality, even though it often lies subterraneously or at a subverbal level in the novel; a great many of her adventures are sexual; but the life of the flesh is faded completely by the glare of the life of the pocketbook; and the incipience of sensuality, its always latent presence, contrasts ironically with the meagerness and abstractness of a sensibility which frantically converts all sense experience into cash value.

We shall continue to speak of ironies in *Moll Flanders*, and as we shall be speaking of them as aspects of the book's internal structure, let us formulate what we mean by the structural function of irony. We shall do so most easily by analogy. A round arch is made up of a number of wedge-shaped blocks, and each of these blocks is pulled earthward in obedience to gravity, but each also exerts a sideways push against its neighbor because of its wedge shape and the weight of other blocks around and over it. If there were only the one pull, freely earthward, the blocks would fall and there would be no arch; but because of the counterforce, acting in the sideways direction, the structure of the arch is defined and preserved. The contrasting significances of an ironic statement or of an ironic situation may be compared with the counteracting stresses that hold the arch up and hold it together—that give it its structure. In *Moll Flanders*, a complex system of ironies or counterstresses holds the book together as a coherent and significant work of art. We may speak of the ironies, then, as "structural." In the example that we have cited, Moll's latent sensuality acts as a counterstress to her devotion to financial abstractions, and the cross-pulls of these two tendencies define Moll and her world meaningfully for us.

To illustrate further, let us follow some of her characteristic mental processes. Here is one chief inflection of her psychology— the reader will find it repeated again and again as he listens to her tale. It appears in her account of her first marriage, her marriage to the younger brother of her seducer. Five years she has been married to him, she has had two children by him, she has known a long and important period (important because she is still very young) of domesticity and marital tenderness and motherhood. How does she tell us of these matters?

> It concerns the story in hand very little to enter into the further particulars . . . only to observe that I had two children by him, and that at the end of the five years he died. He had been really a very good husband to me, and we lived very agreeably together; but as he had not received much from them [the parents], and had in the little time he lived acquired no great matters, so my circumstances were not great, nor was I much mended by the match. Indeed, I had preserved the elder brother's bonds to me to pay me £500, which he offered me for my consent to marry his brother; and this, with what I had saved of the money he formerly gave me, and about as much more by my husband, left me a widow with about £1200 in my pocket.

We know in some degree from this context, and with added conviction from other similar contexts, what Moll means by a "very good husband" and by saying that they lived "very agreeably": the man had enough money to keep Moll from want, he spent money freely enough to maintain her in comfort and in that kind of social respectability which the spending of money guarantees—therefore he was "good" and their life was "agreeable." Any other characterization of this husband or of their marital life we should not be able to guess at; for Moll, simply by her exclusion of any other kind of perception from her story, stringently limits our own imagination of character; and we must judge that Moll has no other perception of character. The phrases "received much," "acquired no great matters," "my circumstances were not great," and "mended by the match," all focus together on one kind of referent: money. And when we find similar phrases in other contexts, we shall expect that "much" and "matters" and "circumstances" and "great" and "mended" (though these words might have immensely different meanings in other books) will have the same common referent again. As Moll uses them, they are very abstract words, colorless little words, words as limited in meaning as a mathematical sign. By their frequency they compose a picture of Moll's mentality and sensibility, so exclusively focused, so narrow and intense, that if (conceivably) we were offered the same description of symptoms in a clinical case history, we should say that it was a picture of a madwoman. But Moll's is not a case history; it is a hypothesis of personality development in an acquisitive world; and in this world Moll is by no means a clinical subject—she is "well adjusted."

What five years of her young womanhood, marriage, domesticity, and motherhood mean to Moll are certain finances, certain bonds amounting to so much, a certain quantity of cash in her pocket. Of her children by this husband, she says,

> My two children were, indeed, taken happily off my hands by my husband's father and mother, and that was all they got by Mrs. Betty.

The statement informs us, with powerful obliquity, that the way to be happy through children is to have them taken off one's hands; it informs us also that children may be useful in settling family debts. With the greatest placidity and aplomb on Moll's part, the children are neatly converted into a shrewd price by which she gets out of a bad bargain with clean skirts. Schematically, what has been happening here is the conversion of all subjective, emotional, and moral experience—implicit in the fact of Moll's five years of marriage and motherhood—into pocket and bank money, into the materially measurable. It is a shocking formula, shocking in its simplicity and abruptness and entireness. It confronts us again with the irony, or system of ironies, that is structural to the book. A great mass of responses that might be expected from the circumstances (marriage, death, birth) is not what is presented; what is presented of that pyramid of human experience, as its only symbol and significance, is a cash sign. And yet another irony is involved: that is the paradox of Moll's superb "sanity," witnessed by her perfect "adjustment" to her world, and her violent abnormality as a representative of the species called human. A person is sane who is socially adapted in his time and his place, in tune with his culture,

furnished with the mental and moral means to meet contingencies
(to "mend" his circumstances, in Moll's phrase, when they need
mending), accepting the values that his society accepts, and
collaborating in their preservation. By these tokens, Moll is
eminently sane. She is a collector of quantities of things and of cash,
for in the world in which she lives, the having of things and of cash
is necessary for survival; it is an expression of the will to live. She
has one thing to sell, in order to obtain them, and that is her sex.
When this commodity fails her, she simply takes the things and the
cash—steals them. In either case, she shows her sanity, her
"adjustment" to her world, her ability to meet all contingencies. In
this sense she is "normal," exhibiting in her activities and attitudes
the social norm of her world; in terms of the full emotional variety
of what we think of as the "human," she is monstrously abnormal.
Her abnormality is her exclusive abstractiveness as a counter of
cash; her subjective life is sunken nearly to a zero.

What will Moll do when she is under severe emotional stress; that
is, when there is nothing in her situation that she can abstract into
numbers, measurements, cash value, and when whatever is left for
her perception to work on is the internal or subjective life of feeling
and emotion? At the crisis of her career, she is taken for thieving,
put into Newgate prison; and Newgate is hell. We have only Moll's
own words for this experience, and how are Moll's words—dictated
by a perceptive apparatus adapted exclusively for enumerating and
calculating—to describe hell for us? Hell, Milton's Satan said, is a
place within the self; that is, it is a subjective place, a place defined
by horror and suffering and deep distress of spirit. In all her other
circumstances, Moll has never failed to describe and define with the
utmost precision such experience as she is capable of. But the hell of
Newgate is "impossible to describe." The impossible description of
this dead end of human suffering she fills up with negatives, words
denying any possibility of description, for she has only negatives
and blank counters for the subjective.

. . . indeed, nothing could be filled with more horror . . . nothing was more odious to me than the company that was there . . . indeed no colours can represent that place to the life.

To get over these impossibilities, the hell of Newgate is expressed by generalized reference to noises and smells (Newgate is most painful because it is not "respectable"; there are loud noises and bad smells here as there are in the slums), and by abstract stereotypes of fiendishness.

> . . . the hellish noise, the roaring, swearing, and clamour, the stench and nastiness, and all the dreadful afflicting things that I saw there . . . ; I thought of nothing night or day, but of gibbets and halters, evil spirits and devils; it is not to be expressed how I was harassed . . .

With the intervention of the minister, Moll says she is "perfectly changed," she becomes "another body." But since her perceptions are limited to their familiar categories of number and quantity, suitable for inventorying gold watches and bonds and purse change, but scarcely suitable for the description of grief or guilt or purity, the heaven of her repentance is as ineffable as the hell of Newgate. "The word eternity," she says,

> represented itself with all its incomprehensible additions, and I had such extended notions of it that I know not how to express them. Among the rest, how absurd did every pleasant thing look!—I mean, that we had counted before—when I reflected that these sordid trifles were the things for which we forfeited eternal felicity.

But immediately, after these weightless matters, these incomprehensible additions and extended notions, Moll and her husband are back at the reckoning, the formulary conversion of death and birth, heaven and hell, into cash.

> Our first business was to compare our stock. He was very honest to me, and told me his stock was pretty good . . . I gave him an account of my stock as faithfully . . . My stock which I had with me was £246 some odd shillings; so that we had £354 between us . . .

With her heart lifted up in gratitude to Providence, Moll plans an irreproachable life, for an irreproachable life is now truly possible: Christian virtue and "stock" have become metaphysically identified, an eternal equation in the mysterious plan of things. From now on, God punches the buttons of this cash-register world, and it is virtue that lies in the till. Most grotesque of ironies: the "sordid trifles," the "pleasant things" that now look so "absurd" to Moll, the things for which she now refuses to forfeit her "eternal felicity," come to her henceforth in greater quantities than ever before, precisely as the sign of grace and redemption, the temporal guarantee of her eternal felicity.

In speaking of the structure of *Moll Flanders* in terms of a hierarchy of ironies—a system of stresses and counterstresses (to return to our figure of the arch) that "hold the book together" in significant unity—we are faced with the need, sooner or later, of making some tentative distinction between what the author might have intended ironically and what actually functions ironically in the book. This question, of the author's deliberate intention, arises particularly in connection with irony; for we think of an author as knowing what he is doing better than another person might know what he is doing, and if he is being elaborately ironic, then—one would assume—he must "intend" at least some of the irony. Irony is "double-talk." But if the author is "sincere" and intends no double-talk, would it not be more consistent usage, on our part, to say that the book is "sincere" in the same sense that the author is sincere, that it contains no double-talk, no ironies?

Let us illustrate this difficulty as it suggests itself in the specifically moralizing portions of *Moll Flanders*. Moll robs a child, comes near to murdering the infant, and moralizes the adventure thus:

> . . . as I did the poor child no harm, I only thought I had given the parents a just reproof for their negligence, in leaving the poor lamb to come home by itself, and it would teach them to take more care another time . . .

She rolls a drunk, after a night spent whoring, comes home to count and weigh her loot, and accompanies her highly satisfactory calculations with moving reflections on the sins which fathers visit upon their children by drunkenness and wenching; she is even inspired to quote Solomon on the foul disease. These reflections are followed by a complacent account of how the adventure, into which she had led the gentleman, had brought him to reform his ways, restored him to the bosom of a loving wife, and secured the happiness of an innocent family. It is to these moralizing thoughts of Moll's that Defoe is undoubtedly referring the reader, in his Author's Preface, when he advises us to make "virtuous and religious uses" of the story. He even mentions, in his Preface, the incident of the robbery of the little girl, and the moral message he associates with this incident is precisely that given it by Moll herself—parents who deck their children in finery and allow them to go to dancing school alone are given a "good memento" of what may ensue; and, generally, the moral that he would have us find in Moll's accounts of her criminal practices is that which Moll (now a reformed soul and "honest" woman at the time of writing her memoirs) is herself always anxious to inculcate. But what, objectively, is the relationship of Moll's moralizing thoughts to her adventures? Her adventures are criminal, but she herself is not a criminal type; she is not a woman of the underworld, but a woman of the bourgeois world; her aspirations are thoroughly middle-class —she wants, above all, economic security and middle-class respectability. She thinks middle-class thoughts; her morality is middle-class morality—platitudinous, stereotypic, a morality suited to the human species in its peculiar aspect as cash calculator, and a morality, therefore, most particularly suitable to the prostitute.

Criminal in action, Moll will have to moralize crime as a social good: and so she does. Her robbery of a child will have prevented many future crimes of this kind; her depredations upon one drunk will have preserved the happiness of many families: all the readers of *Moll Flanders* will have received her benefactions. Moll's moralizing thoughts are the harmonies of the cash-register world in which she lives, for the cash register, like the celestial spheres, has its harmonies too, as the buttons are punched, the mechanism throbs, and the till rolls out. But these harmonies are so divergent from the harmonies of what we know, from our own observations and from the history of ethical ideas, as the spiritually and morally sensitive life, that their meaning in the total context of the book offers itself as ironic meaning: the morality that is preached by Moll is a burlesque of morality.

But if Defoe "intended" Moll's little moral sermons as the message of his book (and he does, in his Author's Preface, so guarantee them for us as his own persuasions), how can they be said to be ironic? We are left with two possibilities. Either *Moll Flanders* is a collection of scandal-sheet anecdotes naïvely patched together with the platitudes that form the morality of an impoverished soul (Defoe's), a "sincere" soul but a confused and degraded one; or *Moll Flanders* is a great novel, coherent in structure, unified and given its shape and significance by a complex system of ironies. The most irreducible fact about the book is that we read it—and reread it—with gusto and marvel. We could not do this if it were the former of our alternatives. That it may be the latter is justified by the analysis it yields itself to, as an ironic structure, and most of all justified by our pleasure in it. Shall we, then, waive the question of Defoe's "intention" and "sincerity"? Speculations as to these apparently can add nothing to the book nor can they take anything from it; the book remains what it is. And we do not have appropriate instruments for analysis of Defoe's intention and sincerity, in the deepest meaning of intention and sincerity. We might guess that a great book could not be written by an impoverished soul, and that imponderable traits of moral sensitivity and prophetic intuition might lie in an author and realize themselves in his book without his recognition of them: these would be guesses. Not guess, but inescapable assurance from the quality of the book, is Defoe's understanding of his creature, Moll, whatever else he might not have recognized or understood in the work that was going on under his own hand as the product of his observant eye and his faculty for clean selection and coherent arrangement. In understanding his creature without the slightest divarication from her movements and her thoughts, he gave to Moll the immense and seminal reality of an Earth Mother, progenitrix of the wasteland, sower of our harvests of technological skills, bombs, gadgets, and the platitudes and stereotypes and absurdities of a morality suitable to a wasteland world.

The Conclusion of *Roxana*

by James R. Sutherland

If *Colonel Jack* shows signs of disintegrating into the loose form
of a picaresque narrative, *The Fortunate Mistress* (published early in
1724, and generally known as *Roxana*) is the most elaborately
constructed of all Defoe's novels. There are more links than usual
between the past and the present, and some of these are highly
important in the development of the events and of the situation in
which Roxana finds herself. Her improvident first husband turns up
again in Paris, a trooper in the service of Louis XIV, but futile as
ever; and, more important, the Dutch merchant who helped her to
sell her jewels and later to escape to Holland becomes more deeply
involved with her, and eventually, after an absence of many years,
comes to England and marries her. All this time Roxana's faithful
maid Amy is either with her or working for her. At first a fairly
neutral character, Amy ends by becoming something a good deal
more significant than a female Man Friday.

Most important of all (for this is a novel in which retribution
becomes the dominant theme) is the reappearance of the children of
Roxana's first marriage. When in the later pages her past begins to
catch up with her and a daughter that she had conveniently
forgotten about for many years begins her relentless pursuit of her, a
tension is engendered that is unlike anything in Defoe's other
stories. The special effect of the concluding section of *Roxana* is a
strongly aroused expectation, a sense of impending discovery and
consequent disaster, just when the heroine appears to be set at last

"The Conclusion of *Roxana*." From James Sutherland, *Daniel Defoe: A Critical
Study*, pp. 205–16 [notes renumbered]. Copyright © 1971 by Houghton Mifflin
Company. Used by permission of the publisher.

on a prosperous course and to have real hopes of living down that notorious past which is quite unknown to her kindly and honorable husband. It seems only a matter of time till the blow will fall; yet when the situation has become desperate and is moving towards a complete exposure and a tragic ending, the narrative comes to a sudden stop, leaving Roxana's story manifestly unfinished. As the book ends, Roxana, now a countess, has retired with her husband to Holland. "Here," she tells us,

> after some few years of flourishing and outwardly happy circum-
> stances, I fell into a dreadful course of calamities, and Amy also; the
> very reverse of our former good days; the blast of Heaven seem'd to
> follow the injury done the poor girl by us both; and I was brought so
> low again that my repentance seem'd to be only the consequence of
> my misery, as my misery was of my crime.

From the first Defoe had been apt to bring his stories to a rather perfunctory conclusion, but here there is no conclusion at all. So obvious was this, that some years after Defoe's death someone gave *Roxana* a new ending in about 30,000 words, in which Roxana is found out, loses her fortune, is imprisoned for debt, and dies in an Amsterdam jail, while her maid Amy (who must by this time have been well over sixty) apparently expires in a hospital as the result of venereal disease.[1]

Why, then, did Defoe fail to finish his own novel in his own way? The crudest explanation would be that the book he had written was already longer than *Moll Flanders* or *Colonel Jack*, and that his publishers had cried, "Hold, enough!" But such an explanation is surely implausible: an experienced writer like Defoe had no need to leave the outcome of Roxana's life history hanging in the air when two or three more paragraphs would have brought it to a genuine conclusion. It is hard to resist the assumption that *Roxana* had got out of hand, and that Defoe didn't know how to finish his own story; or, alternatively, that he knew what must be done but

---

[1] *Roxana* (Shakespeare Head ed., Oxford, 1927–28), ii. 160. The additional matter to *Roxana* will be found in the Bohn reprint (iv. 292–350).

couldn't bring himself to do it. His general pattern in the fiction he had previously written was for a hero or heroine to pass through various adventures and vicissitudes, and at the end to achieve stability and prosperity. This happy ending was sometimes achieved only with a certain amount of moral compromise on the part of the author, who allowed his Captain Singleton and his Moll Flanders to retain their ill-gotten gains, but at the same time indicated that they had turned over a new leaf and attained at least some measure of repentance. It looks as if he had intended a similar rehabilitation for Roxana; for she too shows signs of repentance, and after her marriage to the Dutch merchant appears to be heading for a respectable old age. Yet, when it came to the point, Defoe may have felt unable to ignore the moral consequences.

> King David and King Solomon led rich luxurious lives,
> They spent their money freely on concubines and wives;
> But when old age came creeping on, then both of them felt qualms,
> And Solomon wrote the Proverbs, and David wrote the Psalms.

Those lines represent pretty well the moral situation of Captain Singleton and Moll, although Defoe might have repudiated any such suggestion indignantly. Why, then, does he make an exception of Roxana? For one thing, he almost certainly drew a distinction between the prosperity attributable to successful theft or piracy (wrong, of course, but *comparatively* speaking respectable), and that due to successful whoring. That he made such a distinction is suggested by the behavior of Roxana when she marries her faithful and honorable Dutch merchant. She cannot bear to think (she says) that the wealth her husband had gained by honest trading should be mixed up with her own tainted possessions:

> *Unhappy wretch,* said I to myself, *shall my ill-got wealth, the product of* prosperous lust *and of a vile and vicious life of* whoredom and adultery, *be intermingled with the honest well-gotten estate of this honest gentleman, to be a moth and a caterpiller among it, and bring the judgments of Heaven upon him, and upon what he has, for my sake! Shall my wickedness blast his comforts!*

> *Shall I* be fire in his flax! *and be a means to provoke Heaven to curse his*
> *blessings!* God forbid! *I'll keep them asunder, if it be possible.*

It is Roxana who is speaking, but she is probably expressing Defoe's feelings as much as her own. The fact that her statement is set in italic type is obviously meant to draw the reader's particular attention to it, and the biblical overtones seem more natural to Defoe than to Roxana.[2]

Quite apart, however, from Defoe's own attitude to a life of luxury and lucrative whoring, he had embarked in the later pages of his novel on a course that could only lead to disaster for his heroine. Once he had brought her daughter upon the scene he was committed to a process of retribution, and there was now no escape for Roxana so long as this troublesome girl was still alive. At some point in the course of composition (possibly with a view to achieving even yet some sort of happy ending for Roxana) Defoe seems to have decided that her daughter must be removed from the scene. She could conceivably have died a natural death or have met with a fatal accident; but Defoe chose to have her murdered by the too faithful Amy. The statement in the final sentence of the novel already quoted, that "the blast of Heaven seem'd to follow the injury done the poor girl by us both" refers to the fate of this daughter; but it is symptomatic of the ambiguous nature of the concluding pages that Defoe never states quite clearly that the girl was in fact murdered. The first time that Amy threatens to make away with her, Roxana says that if she ever does such a dreadful thing she will personally see that she hangs for it, and would even cut Amy's throat herself. Some time later Amy tells Roxana that her daughter has found out about her marriage to the Dutch merchant, and that she knows his name and will certainly seek her out. "In the middle of all my amazement," Roxana tells us,

> Amy starts up, and runs about the room like a distracted body; I'll
> put an end to it, that I will; I can't bear it; I must murther her; I'll

kill her, B———,* *and swears by her Maker, in the most serious tone in the* world. . . .

But again she is rebuked by Roxana who forbids her to hurt a hair of her daughter's head, but ends by saying rather feebly, "Well, well, be quiet, and do not talk thus, I can't bear it." Later still, when Roxana has become convinced that her identity (and her past life) are known to her daughter, and is upbraided by Amy for not having allowed her to kill the girl, she says, "I was not for killing the girl yet." This undoubtedly looks ominous; but "yet" almost certainly carries the meaning of "nevertheless," especially as she goes on to say, "I cou'd not bear the thoughts of that neither." At last, when Amy recurs once more to the pressing need to do away with the girl, Roxana finally breaks with her terrible maid, and tells her she will never see her face again.[3]

Defoe has been so careful, on one occasion after another, not to implicate Roxana in the death of her daughter and to make her recoil in horror from the suggestion of it, that it looks as if he had no intention of portraying her as a hardened sinner. Her behavior to the other surviving children of her first marriage, and even to this troublesome daughter, for whom she has made secret provision, is certainly not that of an unnatural mother. On the other hand Roxana takes no steps to *prevent* Amy from carrying out her murderous threat, and to that extent she is culpable. Roxana's attitude is fairly summed up in the lines,

> Thou shalt not kill; but needst not strive
> Officiously to keep alive.

At all events Defoe's handling of this dreadful episode is oddly muted: he may already have realized the terrible impact the girl's murder must have on his story, and have felt that by leaving it indefinite he was doing something to lessen the disastrous effect it would have on the reader's attitude to Roxana. The nearest we

---

* This is the reading of the first edition. I take B——— to stand for "By God!". Some later editions read: "I'll kill the B———" [bitch].

[3] *Ibid.*, ii. 88, 90, 91, 122, 139.

come to being actually told that Amy has carried out her threat is
in a letter from the Quaker lady to Roxana, in which she relates
what Amy had reported to her. After giving the Quaker an account
of how troublesome the girl had been to her mistress by hunting
after her and following her from place to place, Amy had added (as
Roxana tells it) that

> there was an absolute necessity of securing her and removing her
> out-of-the-way; and that, in short, without asking my leave, or
> anybody's leave, she wou'd take care she shou'd trouble her mistress
> (meaning me) no more; and that after Amy had said so, she had
> indeed never heard any more of the girl; so that she suppos'd Amy
> had manag'd it so well as to put an end to it.

The innocent Quaker merely assumed that Amy "had found some
way to perswade her to be quiet and easie," but Roxana had no
illusions about what that way must have been.

> I was struck as with a blast from Heaven at the reading of her letter;
> I fell into a fit of trembling from head to foot; and I ran raving about
> the room like a mad-woman. . . . I threw myself on the bed, and
> cry'd out, *Lord be merciful to me, she has murther'd my child;* and with that
> a flood of tears burst out, and I cry'd vehemently for above an hour.

Anticipating this ghastly event in her rather rambling narrative,
Roxana had already told us that Amy was forming "a more fatal
and wicked design in her head against her; which, indeed, I never
knew till after it was executed, nor durst Amy ever communicate it
to me." The word "fatal" seems to put the issue out of doubt; but
what Amy actually did we are never told.[4]

At what stage Defoe decided that his story was going to include
cold-blooded murder we cannot know. But once he had allowed it
to be committed, all prospects of his usual happy ending became
impossible. In the natural process of events Amy would be
suspected, apprehended, tried, and almost certainly condemned
and hanged at Tyburn. Besides becoming more important as a
fictional character than her mistress while all this was going on, she

[4] *Ibid.,* ii. 152, 137.

would almost inevitably involve Roxana in her fate; for either Roxana would have to give evidence against her maid, or she would have to stand by her, conceal her knowledge of Amy's intentions, and protest her belief in her innocence. In either case Roxana would inevitably sink lower in our estimation; and whichever course she adopted, the fact that the dead girl was her own daughter was bound to come out, with all the attendant exposure of her past. It looks as if Defoe had involved himself in a train of events that he was unwilling to follow to their natural conclusion. He had been careful, as we have seen, to absolve Roxana from any complicity in the death of her daughter; but in developing the powerful situation in which the persistent girl strove to establish that Roxana was her mother he perhaps failed to weigh the consequences of having her murdered. In any event it is hard to resist the conviction that the novel comes to an abrupt end because Defoe's hand was being forced, and the ending he had originally planned was no longer possible. . . .

Much as she may differ from Moll Flanders, Roxana has all of Moll's intelligence; indeed, she probably strikes most readers as having the superior intellect. Whereas Moll gets through life by acting upon impulse and by bold improvisation, Roxana almost never acts hastily, but weighs up each new situation and draws up her plans to deal with it. This cool and calculating approach, and the very frankness with which she describes her motives, make her for most readers a less attractive character than Moll. We first become aware of her formidable mind when she expresses her disgust with her stupid brewer husband. ("Never, ladies, marry a fool; any husband rather than a fool. . . . What is more shocking than for a woman to bring a handsome, comely fellow of a husband into company, and then be oblig'd to blush for him every time she hears him speak? To hear other gentlemen talk sense, and he be able to say nothing? . . . I had now five children by him; the only work (perhaps) that fools are good for.") Equally impressive is the absence of any illusions in Roxana's mind about the sort of life she has been living, and her calm and clear-headed assessment of her own motives. This may be all part of Defoe's determination that the reader shall have no illusions about fornication and adultery; but even if that was his reason for making Roxana examine herself so frequently and find herself wanting, the effect of such passages on the reader is to make him more than ever aware of her intelligence and intellectual honesty. Most striking of all, perhaps, is Roxana's long debate with her Dutch lover, who, having been to bed with her, is anxious to make her an "honest woman," but fails completely in his attempt to marry her. Roxana has now acquired economic independence: why, she asks, should she exchange it for the state of matrimony, in which she and all she possesses would become the property of her husband? This goes far beyond the cry of Congreve's Millamant, "My dear liberty, shall I leave thee?", when she is about to give her hand to Mirabel; and it is characteristic of Roxana (and of Defoe) that it is the economic argument that prevails. Defoe cannot possibly have approved of Roxana "living in sin," and Professor Starr believes that the reader is intended to view her as a woman who is guilty "not merely of fornication but of preaching and promoting it." He points out, too, that Roxana later acknowledges the foolishness and wickedness of the position she has defended on this occasion, and he accordingly disagrees with those who see in her determination to remain free "an extreme statement of Defoe's characteristic feminism." This would be more convincing if Roxana were not so eloquent, and if the Dutchman had anything really substantial to offer in reply. Of course Roxana's is an extreme statement; but it is hard to believe that it was not meant by Defoe to shock his readers into reconsidering the status of women and the inequality to which they were traditionally subjected. "I told him," says Roxana,

> I had, perhaps, differing notions of matrimony from what the receiv'd custom had given us of it; that I thought a woman was a free agent as well as a man, and was born free, and cou'd she manage herself suitably, might enjoy that liberty to as much purpose as the men do; that the laws of matrimony were indeed otherwise, and mankind at this time acted upon quite other principles; and those

such that a woman gave herself entirely away from herself in marriage, and capitulated only to be at best but an upper-servant. . . . That the very nature of the marriage-contract was, in short, nothing but giving up liberty, estate, authority, and every-thing to the man, and the woman was indeed a meer woman ever after, that is to say, a slave.

To this Roxana adds that in her opinion "a woman was as fit to govern and enjoy her own estate, without a man, as a man without a woman; and that, if she had a mind to gratifie herself as to sexes, she might entertain a man, as a man does a mistress." In such passages we are surely listening to the Shavian Defoe, the Defoe who liked to *épater les bourgeois*, who delighted in argument and paradox. But again, so far as Roxana is concerned, the effect of such statements is to impress us with the vigor and independence of her mind, whether we agree with her arguments or reject them.[5]

However we interpret Roxana's determination to keep her liberty, her refusal of the Dutch merchant's offer of marriage was clearly intended by Defoe to be a turning point in her career. It is here that she receives a solemn warning which has been virtually ignored by critics of this novel. When the Dutchman is finally compelled to accept the fact that Roxana will not marry him, he leaves her a letter in which he warns her that her decision will be her ruin, and that she will seriously repent it:

He foretold some fatal things, which, he said, he was well assur'd I shou'd fall into; and that at last I wou'd be ruin'd by a bad husband. . . . This letter stunn'd me: I cou'd not think it possible for anyone that had not dealt with the Devil to write such a letter; for he spoke of some particular things which afterwards were to befal me, with such an assurance that it frighted me before-hand; and when those things did come to pass, I was perswaded he had some more than human knowledge. . . .[6]

    [5] *Roxana*, 4f., 7; Congreve, *The Way of the World*, Act IV, Sc. i (Mermaid ed., p. 378); Starr, *Defoe and Spiritual Autobiography*, p. 176; *Roxana*, i. 171f.
    [6] *Ibid.*, i. 186.

In another writer this might not mean very much; but in Defoe, with his frequently expressed belief in predictions, omens, and other occult manifestations, it is clearly meant to be taken seriously. What, then, are we to make of the Dutchman's prediction that Roxana would be "ruined by a bad husband"? Unless this is another reference to the wretched brewer (who was by this time dead, but who had begotten the daughter who was eventually to prove so fatal to Roxana's peace of mind), it looks as if at this point in the composition of his story Defoe had envisaged a different sort of fate for his heroine. Once again we seem to have come upon one of those loose ends that are so common in Defoe's fiction, and to which there seems to be no better answer than Whitman's

> Do I contradict myself?
> Very well then I contradict myself,
> (I am large, I contain multitudes.)

Defoe's *Journal of the Plague Year* and the Modern Urban Experience

by W. Austin Flanders

No criticism of Defoe's *Journal of the Plague Year* has quite explained the source of its imaginative appeal to the modern reader or of the plague year to Defoe himself, largely because works pretending to documentary accuracy as their principal foundation have seldom invited reading as works of imaginative literature. Pepy's *Diary*, Gibbon's *History*, and Defoe's *Journal* are important examples of such works in the literature of the Restoration and eighteenth century. Much recent commentary on Defoe's work has centered on its accuracy as an historical document.[1] I would like to examine it from a literary point of view and to argue that it is *primarily* concerned neither with the religious debate over the plague's providential nature nor with actual history, but rather with certain aspects of eighteenth-century psychological and social experience common to all of Defoe's fiction and central to his most successful works.

"Defoe's *Journal of the Plague Year* and the Modern Urban Experience." From *The Centennial Review*, 16 (Fall 1972), 328–48.

[1] See, for example, F. Bastian, "Defoe's *Journal of the Plague Year* Reconsidered," *Review of English Studies*, n.s. 16 (1965), 151–73; Manuel Schonhorn, "Defoe's *Journal of the Plague Year*: Topography and Intention," *Review of English Studies*, n.s. 19 (1968), 387–402; and the introduction and notes to Louis Landa's edition of *A Journal of the Plague Year* (London, 1969). For discussions based on analysis of the *Journal's* religious debate, see E. Zimmerman, "H. F.'s Meditations: *A Journal of the Plague Year*," *PLMA*, 87 (1972), 417–23 and G. A. Starr, *Defoe and Casuistry* (Princeton, 1971), both of which suggest that its interest is not primarily that of an historical document.

In this light, the *Journal* may be viewed as a reflection of Defoe's experience of life as he perceived it in the 1720's projected through an account of the plague of 1664. Although it lacks plot and characters of a novelistic sort, it is more akin to historical fiction than to history[2] and shares the chief concerns of the eighteenth-century novel and of other important literature of the period. The continuing appeal of the work cannot lie in the limited formal success of the composition but must be found in its application to the modern reader's experience of life. It is Defoe's triumph in the *Journal* to have captured the essence of the psychological experience of urban life under circumstances of composition which could easily have produced merely ephemeral journalism. No really successful work can ever emerge from writing which does not engage the imaginative energies and emotional commitment of the author. Although there was a threat of plague at the time Defoe wrote the *Journal*, it was relatively remote, and has been ever since. We must, I believe, look elsewhere than to the immediate circumstances of composition for a key to its continuing vitality.

What was likely to have been the perspective of Defoe and his audience on the events he describes in the *Journal*? The work itself gives us an important clue:

> It must not be forgot here, that the City and Suburbs were prodigiously full of People, at the time of this Visitation, I mean, at the time that it began; for tho' I have liv'd to see a farther Encrease, and mighty Throngs of People settling in *London*, more than ever, yet we had always a Notion, that the Numbers of People, which the Wars being over, the Armies disbanded, and the Royal Family and the Monarchy being restor'd, had flock'd to *London*, to settle into Business; or to depend upon, and attend the Court for Rewards of Services, Preferments, *and the like*, was such, that the Town was computed to have in it above a hundred thousand people more than ever it held before; nay, some took upon them to say, it had twice as many, because all the ruin'd Families of the royal Party, flock'd

---

[2] Bastian, in the article cited above, classifies the work primarily as history on the basis of his identification of the historical accuracy of its details. Landa discusses the genre of the *Journal* in his introduction, pp. xxxvi ff.

> hither: All the old Soldiers set up Trades here, and abundance of
> Families settled here; again, the Court brought with them a great
> Flux of Pride, and new Fashions; All People were grown gay and
> luxurious; and the Joy of the Restoration had brought a vast many
> families to *London*.
>
> I often thought, that as *Jerusalem* was besieg'd by the *Romans*, when
> the *Jews* were assembled together, to celebrate the Passover, by
> which means, an incredible Number of People were surpriz'd there,
> who would otherwise have been in other Countries: So the Plague
> entred *London*, when an incredible Increase of People had hap-
> pened. . . .[3]

In this appeal to the reader not to forget the circumstances of urban
crowding, the narrator's remark that he has "liv'd to see . . .
mighty Throngs of People settling in *London*, more than ever" is an
appeal to the sensibilities of his urban audience and gives Defoe's
view of the basic conditions of plague. The vast shift in the quality
of urban life that took place between the Renaissance and 1800 has
been amply documented,[4] it explains Defoe's evocation of a
pervasive sense of numbers and oppressive overcrowding in the
passage above. Unprecedented in the history of mankind other than
in imperial Rome, this shift provided a constant source of concern
for eighteenth-century British authors who were of course, quick to
see the Roman parallel.

The deleterious effect of such change on the quality of moral and
social life is a primary concern in early eighteenth-century literature. Hogarth's pictures of London in the first half of the century
concretize pervasive moral depravity and sudden death in terms not
too different in tone from those of Juvenal's third satire. For Defoe
and his reader, much of the force of the central situation in the

---

[3] Landa, *op. cit.*, p. 18. All quotations of the *Journal* are from this edition; further
page references given in parentheses in the text.

[4] In *London Life in the XVIIIth Century* (New York, 1925), Dorothy George said,
"That sense of sudden and unmanageable growth—of invasion by hordes of
workers who create new problems—dates for London from the end of the sixteenth
century" (p. 1). She observes that in the 17th and 18th centuries "there were
repeated periods of distress owing to dislocating transitions from peace to war and
war to peace, to trade crises and to times of dearth and epidemics" (p. 20).

Journal undoubtedly lay in its recognition of the anxieties generated by a sense of the precariousness of individual life in the midst of rapid urban expansion. The year 1722, "the wars being over," was a year of peace, as was 1664; The Peace of Utrecht was an event of recent memory and it was in English domestic life the time of "the growth of political stability," to use J. H. Plumb's words, under Walpole. Yet at the time of the *Journal's* publication, the major literary figures were expressing more and more discontent with the quality of contemporary life in London. In spite of much gaiety and affluence, the possibility of sudden and irrational visitations of death has much immediacy for Defoe and engrosses him entirely. Spectres of annihilation are recurrent in the literature of the Restoration and eighteenth century; apocalyptic forebodings are common to some of the greatest works of the age—*The Hind and the Panther*, the *Dunciad*, and Gibbon's *History*. These works and Defoe's *Journal* give expression to a sense of the tenuousness of life and moral order, to anxiety at witnessing the spectacle of civilization. For Defoe, apparently, a view of the great plague of the previous century seemed appropriate as an embodiment of a state of mind generated by the urban life of his own time.

Dread and anxiety are the central emotions examined in the work. In the early pages of the *Journal* Defoe discusses the alternations of hope and fear that beset Londoners after the first threat of plague and conveys a growing sense of insecurity as the plague visibly worsens. One does not have to have lived under a threat of plague to empathize with this feeling; it is a principal emotional condition of city life and is widely exploited in popular literature written for the now-pervasive urban mentality. Contemporary journalistic works such as popular science fiction or the "new journalism" coverage of social and moral disasters exploit this dread of sudden, violent death and widespread social disintegration. They reveal the connections between plague-ridden London of the seventeenth century and the modern experience of life. Defoe explicitly points to the *urban* condition as the heart of the situation he describes, not the existence of disease itself. As in the long passage quoted above, Defoe recurrently parallels London during the plague to a city besieged in wartime: "several *Dutch* Merchants were particularly remarkable, who kept their Houses like little Garrisons besieged." (p. 55) Only when cities grow to size and affluence does organized warfare on a large scale become feasible and only then does a sense of the impingement of irrational and violent death on a large scale occur. That the city draws and magnifies many inhumane forces of civilization is a commonplace among historians and sociologists. The imaginative achievement of Defoe's work is to grasp this tendency of city life and to create a work which calls on the common store of urban experience for its responses. He demonstrates the idea, as Lewis Mumford puts it, that "the human dialogue, the drama, the living circle of mates and associates, the society of friends . . . sustain the growth and reproduction of human culture, and without them the whole elaborate structure becomes meaningless—indeed actively hostile to the purposes of life." [5] When the "living circle" breaks, death threatens its triumph.

Defoe traces the process by which urban dwellers, after constant confrontation with plague victims, develop a sense of alienation from and hostility to others—the anonymous "them" with whom we are familiar today. As the plague spreads, concern for the plight of others decreases:

> People might be heard even into the Streets as we pass'd along, calling upon God for Mercy, thro' Jesus Christ, *and saying,* I have been a Thief, I have been an Adulterer, I have been a Murderer, and the like; and none durst stop to make the least Inquiry into such Things, or to administer Comfort to the poor Creatures, that in the Anguish both of Soul and Body thus cry'd out. (p. 34)

Increasing indifference to others is a central moral issue in the *Journal.* Those "who kept themselves retired and reserv'd, generally escap'd the Contagion," the narrator tells us. (p. 12) Those who dare to communicate with the sick or to live a free social or business

[5] Lewis Mumford, *The City in History* (New York, 1961), pp. 569–70.

life were in extreme danger of infection and the Londoners become mortally afraid of contact with others. It is only with the "safe" that one dares communicate, although even this precaution fails as conditions worsen: "Here also I ought to leave a farther Remark for the use of Posterity, concerning the Manner of Peoples infecting one another; namely, that it was not the sick People only, from whom the Plague was immediately receiv'd by others that were sound, but THE WELL." (p. 190) A universal fear of human contact is the creeping moral and psychological malady which Defoe chronicles. A common feature of city life, plague or no, this fear is one which Defoe can expect to communicate almost effortlessly. Speaking of the psychological effects of urban life, the sociologist Georg Simmel remarked that the

> mental attitude of metropolitans toward one another we may designate, from a formal point of view, as reserve. If . . . inner reactions were responses to the continuous external contacts with innumerable people . . . one would be completely atomized internally and come to an unimaginable psychic state. . . . The inner aspect of this outer reserve is not only indifference, but, more often than we are aware, it is a slight aversion, a mutual strangeness and repulsion, which will break into hatred and fight at the moment of a closer contact. . . . A latent antipathy and the preparative stage of practical antagonism effect the distances and aversions without which this mode of life could not be led.[6]

Simmel's remarks help to clarify the psychological basis of the chronicle of the plague year and to explain its immediacy to the modern urban dweller who has walked down city streets trying to keep himself aloof from feared human contact.

In the plague year the "preparatory stage of practical antagonism" which Simmel describes becomes the aggressive hostility which Defoe shows as one of the results of the crisis. One of the narrator's anecdotes presents incomprehensible, irrationally destructive behavior generated by stress. Some dissolute gentlemen in

[6] Georg Simmel, "The Metropolis and Mental Life," in *The Sociology of Georg Simmel*, tr. and ed. by Kurt H. Wolff (New York, 1950), pp. 415–16.

a tavern confront a man who has just lost his entire family to the common scourge:

> These Gentlemen being something disturb'd with the Clutter of bringing the poor Gentleman into the House, as above, were first angry, and very high with the Master of the House, for suffering such a Fellow, as they call'd him, to be brought out of the Grave into their House; but being answered, that the Man was a Neighbour, and that he was sound, but overwhelmed with the Calamity of his Family, and the like, they turned their Anger into ridiculing the Man, and his Sorrow for his Wife and Children; taunted him with want of Courage to leap into the great Pit, and go to Heaven, as they jeeringly express'd it, along with them, adding some very profane, and even blasphemous Expressions. (p. 64)

Such behavior is heightened in the account of another incident in which a plague victim

> was going along the Street, raving mad to be sure, and singing, the People only said, he was drunk; but he himself said, he had the Plague upon him, which, it seems, was true; and meeting this Gentlewoman, he would kiss her; she was terribly frighted as he was only a rude Fellow, and she run from him, but the Street being very thin of People, there was no body near enough to help her: When she saw he would overtake her, she turn'd, and gave him a Thrust so forcibly, he being but weak, and push'd him down backward: But very unhappily, she being so near, he caught hold of her, and pull'd her down also; and getting up first, master'd her, and kiss'd her; and which was worst of all, when he had done, told her he had the Plague, and why should not she have it as well as he. (p. 160)

In the fears evoked by such incidents lies much of the imaginative appeal of Defoe's work, rather than in the accuracy of the historical reconstruction of events. One does not have to have lived under threat of plague to understand without question the emotions of aggressors or victims in these situations. Such behavior recalls the ceaseless acts of vandalism and violence which plague modern urban life. The fear of the night, supposedly overcome in civilization by the light of reason, reasserts itself: "already People had, as it were by a general Consent, taken up the Custom of not going out of Doors after Sun-set." (p. 12) John Gay's advice to the city dweller in *Trivia* is to be aloof and cautious, especially at night—advice enforced by the bullies' threat in *The Mohocks*:

> We will scower the Town,
> Knock the Constable down,
> Put the Watch and the Beadle to flight:
> We'll force all we meet
> To kneel down at our feet,
> And own this great Prince of the Night.[7]

Gay's rather insouciant detailing of city fears in his works becomes in Defoe's *Journal* a chronicle of horror.

II

Irrational aggression is closely related to another distortion of the urban mentality—the susceptibility to superstition in the face of contrary evidence. Defoe's age prided itself on its rationality and its understanding of natural causes. Granted, the mass of people in any age do not hold an intellectual view of life, yet for Defoe and his readers resorting to astrologers and seers for explanation of the plague was regressive, much as the irruption of violence among neighbors is retrograde in any civilized society. Defoe assumes that his readers will share his disdain for soothsayers and quacks, if only for religous reasons. The narrator admits that he too was affected by "portents" in the heavens, but goes on to add that he knows "natural Causes are assign'd by the Astronomers for such Things." He is aware of a disintegration of good sense among the populace:

> The Apprehensions of the People, were likewise strangely en-creas'd by the Error of the Times; in which, I think, the People, from what Principle I cannot imagine, were more addicted to Prophesies and Astrological Conjurations, Dreams and old Wives Tales, than ever they were before or since. . . . (pp. 20–21)

[7] In *The Poetical Works of John Gay*, ed. G. C. Faber (London, 1926), p. 315.

Thus one more benefit of civilization disintegrates under the pressures of urban disorder. The belief in science which made the technology for urban development possible becomes powerless to overcome the mental disturbance resulting from that development. This kind of atavistic superstition recurs under the pressure of urban life today, as illustrated by widespread faith in astrology and the occult among those most lacking in a sense of security in the values of contemporary civilization.

Another result of moral and social disorder is the perversion of the privacy and often beneficial anonymity of city life into an extreme of isolation and imprisonment. One of the stratagems for escaping infection is withdrawal into a protected insular environment—an alternative, Defoe makes clear, open only to the rich. On one of his walking tours of the city, the narrator meets a poor waterman who acquaints him with some of the contrivances for avoiding contact with the sick. The waterman points to the number of ships anchored in the Thames and says, *"All those Ships have Families on board, of their Merchants and Owners, and such like, who have lock'd themselves up, and live on board, close shut in, for fear of the Infection."* (p. 107) The narrator comments:

> I cannot guess at the Number of Ships, but I think there must be several Hundreds of Sail; and I could not but applaud the Contrivance, for ten thousand People, and more, who attended Ship Affairs, were certainly sheltered here from the Violence of the Contagion, and liv'd very safe and very easy. (p. 111)

A better illustration of urban dwelling patterns among the upper classes could scarcely be given, nor is Defoe silent on the much worse position of the poor, who have not the resources thus to isolate themselves from the common lot:

> As the richer Sort got into Ships, so the lower Rank got into Hoys, Smacks, Lighters, and Fishing-boats; and many, especially Watermen, lay in their Boats; but those made sad Work of it, especially the latter, for going about for Provision, and perhaps to get their Subsistence, the Infection got in among them and made a fearful

> Havock; many of the Watermen died alone in their Wherries, as
> they rid at their Roads, as well above-Bridge as below, and were not
> found sometimes till they were not in Condition for any Body to
> touch or come near them. (pp. 114–115)

Earlier in discussing the medicinal precautions used against infection, the narrator had remarked that "the Poor cou'd not do even
these things, and they went at all Hazards." (p. 78) For the poor,
we see, the conditions of urban life are least beneficial; under the
threat of hard times, they go under first, and go under in numbers
that exceed those of the rich.[8] But we may understand that the
isolation of the rich is no blessing either, for they are much limited
under these circumstances; their isolation is preferable to death, but
is in a sense its precursor—a *memento mori* prefiguring final
entombment.

Defoe's persistent concern with the economic consequences of the
plague is fundamentally a concern with the consequences of urban
capitalism.[9] They are exactly those of an economic depression, a
phenomenon which occurs in a capitalistic economy with as little
apparent reason as disease itself. The fear of economic collapse,
both personal and social, was ever-present to the minds of
eighteenth-century businessmen and speculators. The collapse of
the South-Sea Bubble in 1720[10]—preceding the publication of the

[8] Landa quotes Nathaniel Hodges' *Loimologia* (1720): " '. . . it is incredible to
think how the Plague raged amongst the common people, insomuch that it came
by some to be called the Poors Plague' " (Landa, p. 273, n. 5).

[9] The connection between carrying on business and spreading plague is a
constant one in the *Journal* and reveals how the circumstances of the capitalistic
economy are closely interwoven in the fabric of Defoe's account of the advance and
effects of the disease. Maximillian Novak largely ignores the *Journal* in his *Economics
and the Fiction of Defoe* (Berkeley, 1962), other than to note Defoe's sympathy for the
poor.

[10] In *Daniel Defoe: Citizen of the Modern World*, J. R. Moore says that Defoe
"apparently visited Paris to observe the Mississippi craze" in the summer of 1720
(p. 354; see also pp. 292–93). In the Mississippi Bubble in Paris there was an
economic scare parallel to that following the collapse of the South Sea Bubble in
1720. A report to Parliament by a committee of the House of Commons concerning
the South Sea Bubble was made in February, 1721. The date of the *Journal* is 17
March, 1722.

Journal by little over a year—provides a parallel to the plague and must have struck as much terror into the hearts of its victims as would the advent of a fatal disease. Defoe's images of the desolation of economic activity in London during the plague provide some of the *Journal*'s most vivid moments—as in the much-cited anecdote about the stolen hats. We are told that "all Trades being stopt, Employment ceased; the Labour, and by that, the Bread of the Poor were cut off." The narrator lists the trades halted and comments: *"The Masters of those perhaps might live upon their Substance; but the Traders were Universally at a Stop, and consequently all their Work-men discharged."* (p. 95)

> All Families retrench'd their living as much as possible, as well those that fled, as those that stay'd; so that an innumerable Multitude of Footmen, Serving Men, Shop-keepers, Journey-men, Merchants-Book-keepers, and such Sort of People and especially poor Maid Servants were turn'd off, and left Friendless and Helpless without Employment, and without Habitation; and this was really a dismal Article. (p. 95)

Many, he continues, "might be said to perish, not by the Infection it self, but by the Consequence of it; indeed, namely, by Hunger and Distress, and the Want of all Things." (p. 96).

One need only read descriptions of the state of the urban poor in the time to see the immediacy with which this account must have struck the Londoner in 1722.[11] Defoe emphasizes the role of voluntary charity in alleviating suffering and in averting riots and disorders during the plague. Here he touches upon one of the chief social problems faced by the eighteenth century after the charities administered by the medieval church had all but disappeared, leaving a gap in society of dismal consequences for the quality of

[11] See, for example, D. George's chapter "Parish Children and Poor Apprentices" (pp. 215 ff.) or G. M. Trevelyan's *Illustrated English Social History*, III (Harmondsworth, 1964), p. 94, both of which discuss the state of poor children. Trevelyan speaks of "the sight of babes lying descrtcd by the roadside." Apprentices and servants, as Defoe says, were especial sufferers of the effects of economic disorders. Avoiding the precarious position of maid-servant is one of the chief preoccupations of Moll Flanders and Roxana.

urban life.[12] In the *Journal* Defoe shows how the poor—ignorant, pressed by necessity, yet heedless of the dangers of their condition—multiply their own evils and those of society. The narrator observes that the "adventurous Conduct of the Poor was that which brought the Plague among them in a most furious manner, and this join'd to the Distress of their Circumstances, when taken, was the reason why they died so by Heaps." (p. 210) We learn that

> Where they could get Employment they push'd into any kind of Business, the most dangerous and the most liable to Infection; and if they were spoken to, their Answer would be, *I must trust to God for that; if I am taken, then I am provided for, and there is an End of me,* and the like: OR THUS, *Why, What must I do? I can't starve, I had as good have the Plague as perish for want. I have no Work, what could I do? I must do this or beg:* (p. 210)

The language here—*"if I am taken," "Why, What must I do? I can't starve"*—parallels the situation of the poor with that of the criminal who steals for bread and accepts crime and prostitution as means of survival—a key situation in Defoe's fiction. From his personal experience as a businessman, Defoe knew the possible effects of individual capitalism upon the city dweller. Once the economic system comes under stress, it is *sauve qui peut,* and only the securely affluent or the extraordinarily resourceful can make themselves immune to the worst consequences of disorder. This is a situation which Fielding explores in Captain Booth's helplessness once he sinks into poverty.

Having presented London under the plague, and, by extension, implied his view of city life in general, Defoe offers pastoral life as an alternative. The story of the three poor men involves not only a physical escape from the city but the discovery of an alternative to

---

[12] In *Madness and Civilization* (tr. Richard Howard, New York, 1971), Michel Foucault discusses methods of confining the "irresponsible" poor in workhouses as a corollary of the incarceration of equally socially useless "madmen." Foucault sees the "invention of a site of constraint, where morality castigates by means of administrative enforcement" as a significant creation of bourgeois society (p. 60). Defoe, of course, frequently questions the efficacy or justice of the English methods for dealing with the poor.

economic individualism. The biscuit-baker, sail-maker and joiner who escape London meet with difficulties, but they are difficulties principally occasioned by the hostility of country dwellers to men from the city and to their poverty, difficulties which they overcome through diligence and cooperation. The first thing they find they must do is pool their resources: "The Joyner had a small Bag of Tools, such as might be useful if he should get any Work abroad, as well for their Subsistence as his own: What Money they had, they brought all into one publick Stock, and thus they began their Journey." (p. 127) Later on the group of exiles cooperate to build a rude house in which they manage to survive the ravages of hardship. This episode is on the whole a happy one; it shows that good sense and resolution can, if one can escape London, save him from disaster. Toward the end of the *Journal* the narrator comments on the susceptibility of the city to plague:

> The Plague like a great Fire, if a few Houses only are contiguous where it happens, can only burn a few Houses; or if it begins in a single, or as we call it a lone House, can only burn that lone House where it begins: But if it begins in a close built Town, or City, and gets a Head, there its Fury encreases, it rages over the whole Place, and consumes all it can reach. (p. 198)

He concludes *"that the best Physick against the Plague is to run away from it."* (pp. 197–98) Although a retreat to the countryside is the narrator's alternative to infection, he does not heed his own conclusion and remains in the city. His presence there is a condition of the narrative, of course, but more important to Defoe's meaning is the moral stance emerging in his refusal of the pastoral refuge that was becoming increasingly attractive to British poets throughout the eighteenth century. Why he does not leave provides a key to understanding the moral, as distinct from theological, concerns in the *Journal* and the work's debate over the proper interpretation of the plague.

Defoe can be characterized as an apologist for the values of the mercantile mind and the commercial middle class, especially on the strength of his non-fiction. He may also be considered outstanding among writers who exhibit the values of the bourgeois journalist, for whom literature is merely a commodity. In placing him among his dunces, Pope evidently thought him such. However, in his fiction, far from being an unthinking apologist for capitalism, Defoe persistently questions its moral tendencies.[13] In *A Journal of the Plague Year* this questioning gives rise to the repeated theme of examination of conscience. The moral questions raised, played out against the background of the decay of faith in the age of developing scientific naturalism, are intensified and forced on the individual by the problems of urban life. The character of H. F. and his qualms of conscience reflect the collapse of a sense of moral stability in the social environment.

III

An insistent moral issue confronting the city dweller in modern times is the alienation from and hostility to others which it occasions. Should one isolate himself within a privileged confine within the city, ignoring the suffering and degradation around him; should one escape to suburbia outside the city; or should he more fully accept his brotherhood with others and remain to accept responsibility for the evils which press upon them? Defoe raises this question as a response to the moral issues revealed by the relationships of individuals under urban capitalism. These relationships reveal the failing authority of a concept that had been accepted for centuries—the brotherhood of man under God—and

---

[13] For an example of Defoe's doubts in his non-fiction as well, see *The Complete English Tradesman* (New York, 1969), I, p. 234:

> Custom indeed has driven us beyond the limits of our morals in many things, which trade makes necessary, and which we cannot now avoid; so that if we must pretend to go back to the literal sense of the command, if our yea must be yea, and our nay nay; if no man must go beyond, or defraud his neighbour; if our conversation must be without covetousness, and the like, why then we must shut up shop, and leave off trade. . . .

the growing operative conviction that society is a conglomeration of atomistic individuals. The plague throws these questions into acute relief through the accentuation of the conditions of urban life as cited above.[14]

The struggle between dehumanization and humanistic moral values emerges in the *Journal* in many ways. The narrator vacillates between contempt and pity for the poor. As Landa points out,[15] H. F. is free from immediate personal responsibility to others because he has no family; that is, he is free to contemplate the moral question of his obligation to other people in a rather pure form. However, as a man of business, he can be expected to consider the plague from an exclusively economic point of view; his fascination with statistics reveals his tendency to quantify the problem. We hear the voice of the secure bourgeois in these remarks on the "lavishness" of the poor:

> But it was impossible to beat any thing into the Heads of the Poor, they went on with the usual Impetuosity of their Tempers full of Outcries and Lamentations when taken, but madly careless of themselves, Fool-hardy and obstinate, while they were well. . . . I cannot say, I could observe one jot of better Husbandry among them, I mean the labouring Poor, while they were well and getting Money, than there was before, but as lavish, as extravagant, and as thoughtless for to-morrow as ever; so that when they came to be taken sick, they were immediately in the utmost Distress as well for want, as for Sickness, as well for lack of Food, as lack of Health. (pp. 209–10)

This censure is tempered by his awareness of the "Misery of the Poor" with which he sympathizes and he praises "the charitable Assistance that some pious People daily gave to such." (p. 210) In portraying such ambivalence Defoe perceptively records the strug-

---

[14] See Landa's discussion of the conflict of secular and religious values in his introduction, pp. xviii ff. In his chapter " 'Robinson Crusoe': Individualism and the Novel," in *Rise of the Novel* (Berkeley, 1959), Ian Watt discusses the centrality of the moral problems of economic individualism to the novel.

[15] Landa, p. xxxi.

gle on the part of the bourgeois individualist between scorn and humanistic sympathy for the moral consequences of poverty. He is not, apparently, conscious of representing such a conflict, but it occurs so frequently in his other fiction that it seems to have been almost an obsession with him.[16] In the *Journal*, H. F. is on the whole more sympathetic than censorious.

This moral ambivalence parallels the narrator's conflict over whether or not to leave the city. If he leaves he will no doubt escape the disease but will suffer economically by abandoning his business holdings. He decides to stay after "Providence" communicates a message to him through Biblical divination. He feels, he says, that he should trust to God to preserve him, even though his brother, "a very Religious Man himself," (p. 11) advises him to leave. The religious question is in effect left open here since apparently there is religious authority on both sides and the economic motive is the operative one; after his dispute with his brother, divination provides H. F. with a convenient justification for his choice. However, in staying, he provides himself with the knowledge with which to understand and evaluate the moral issues raised by the plague. There is in the decision a spiritual and moral component which later events confirm, although subsequent pages express further wavering of his developing feelings of moral responsibility. The ambiguity of his attitude as a bourgeois is revealed when he is called upon by the municipal authorities (whom he praises highly for their sense of duty) to be an examiner of the houses of the sick, a task that devolves on him because he has remained in London. Using his position of economic privilege, he buys off:

> I got myself discharg'd of the dangerous Office I was in, as soon as I cou'd get another admitted, who had obtain'd for a little Money to accept of it; and so, instead of serving the two Months, which was directed, I was not above three Weeks in it; and a great while too,

---

[16] See Defoe's consideration of the proper view of Moll Flanders' criminal activities or of the criminality of the young Colonel Jack. Defoe generally, I think, denotes more sympathy than contempt for the poor and tends to excuse if not condone their desperate behavior.

> considering it was in the Month of *August,* at which time the
> Distemper began to rage with great Violence at our end of the
> Town. (p. 169)

Here the narrator has used his economic advantage to avoid
contamination and thereby has exposed another to it. In his
statement on the irresponsibility of the Court (a gesture of contempt
for the Stuarts, no doubt) we see that he does not believe in
avoiding such responsibilities:

> the Court removed early . . . and went to *Oxford,* where it pleas'd
> God to preserve them; and the Distemper did not, *as I heard of,* so
> much as touch them; for which I cannot say, that I ever saw they
> shew'd any great Token of Thankfulness, and hardly any thing of
> Reformation, tho' they did not want being told that their crying
> Vices might, without Breach of Charity, be said to have gone far, in
> bringing that terrible Judgment upon the whole Nation. (pp. 15–16)

This contempt for the Court is echoed in the narrator's condemna-
tion of the Anglican clergy's evasion of responsibility. In such
passages we see Defoe's ambivalent feelings about his moral
relationships. Where economic well-being and self-preservation are
paramount, Defoe seems to anticipate modern attitudes of indifference towards one's neighbors, especially obvious in cities; on the
other hand, when he asserts the duties of men to their fellows, he
implies the view that responsibility for one's brother sufferers is a
spiritual duty, a way to avoid "bringing . . . terrible Judgment
upon the whole Nation."

The sympathetic, curious narrator is unlike others who irre-
sponsibly lapse into irrationality or desert their homes. By staying
in the city, he has acquired for himself moral awareness which
would not have been granted by flight. He wants to know the
situation, to interpret it, to learn from it; he wants to be able to
communicate useful advice and thereby to improve the state of
national life. He could have stayed shut up in his house, but over
and over again he goes out to witness the economic havoc around
him and to see such sights as the Great Pit at Aldgate.

> . . . I could not prevail upon my unsatisfy'd Curiosity to stay within
> entirely my self; and tho' I generally came frighted and terrified

> Home, yet I cou'd not restrain. . . . In these Walks I had many dismal Scenes before my Eyes, as particularly of Persons falling dead in the Streets, terrible Shrieks and Skreekings of Women. . . . Passing thro' *Token-House-Yard in Lothbury*, of a sudden a Casement violently opened just over my Head, and a Woman gave three frightful Skreetches and then cry'd, *Oh! Death, Death, Death!* in a most inimitable Tone, and which struck me with Horror and a Chilness, in my very Blood. (pp. 80–81)

In spite of the urge to economic self-preservation which kept him in London, H. F. refuses to shut himself out from the knowledge which generates sympathy. In the episode concerning the poor waterman, Defoe accurately connects the spreading infection with the loss of charity. The narrator gives the poor man a few shillings and the waterman agrees to row him to see the boats on the river, saying,

> Well Sir, . . . as your Charity has been mov'd to pity me and my poor Family; sure you cannot have so little pity left, as to put your self into my Boat if you were not Sound in Health, which would be nothing less than killing me, and ruining my whole Family. (p. 111)

Here the charitable frame of mind is shown to be essential to saving others from plague; it is implied throughout that the refusal to give in to madness, hysteria and hardness of heart preserves H. F. from the plague. He is—providentially, as he sees it—preserved to give to others his view of the moral state of urban life. The Lord Mayor and others who remain to do their civic duty are contrasted to the Court and the mercenary physicians and clergymen who desert—as the narrator is contrasted to those of hardened heart. H. F. wants to convey the appropriateness of "Charity and Kindness in Remembrance of the past Calamity." (p. 238)

In his discussion of the *Journal*, Manuel Schonhorn asserts that "throughout the experience, Defoe's London [during the plague] has triumphantly asserted its illustrious qualities." [17] Building his view on the supposed political role of the work in encouraging confidence in public life, he finds it an optimistic and encouraging

---

[17] Schonhorn, p. 397.

view of the potentialities of urban society. While it may be true that
Defoe is seeing everything "in the best possible light," [18] in my
opinion he does not present an encouraging view of London. The
narrator comments rather pessimistically on life in the city after the
plague:

> I wish I cou'd say, that as the City had a new Face, so the
> Manners of the People had a new Appearance: I doubt not but there
> were many that retain'd a sincere Sense of their Deliverance, and
> that were heartily thankful to that sovereign Hand, that had
> protected them in so dangerous a Time: it would be very uncharita-
> ble to judge otherwise in a City so populous, and where the People
> were so devout, as they were here in the Time of the Visitation itself;
> but except what of this was to be found in particular Families, and
> Faces, it must be acknowledg'd that the general Practice of the
> People was just as it was before, and very little Difference was to be
> seen.
>
> Some indeed said Things were worse, that the Morals of the
> People declin'd from this very time; that the People harden'd by the
> Danger they had been in, like Sea-men after a Storm is over, were
> more wicked and more stupid, more bold and hardened in their
> Vices and Immoralities than they were before; but I will not carry it
> so far neither. . . . (p. 229)

In refusing to praise the behavior of "the People" while enter-
taining a very negative opinion of them, the narrator expresses a
dark view of the quality of contemporary life. An echo of
Abraham's pleading with the Lord for the cities of the plain can be
heard in the words "it would be very uncharitable to judge
otherwise in a City so Populous." Defoe was no doubt aware that
Abraham's hopes were not answered.

The narrator's refusal to give up a providential view of the
plague reflects the struggle of the seventeenth and eighteenth
centuries to retain a humanistic view of the social community.
Throughout the *Journal* he vacillates between understanding the
plague as a purely naturalistic phenomenon and ascribing to it and

[18] Schonhorn, p. 398.

its consequences a moral significance, although the opposition of interpretations does not surface as a conscious intellectual dichotomy. One of the results of the economic and technological emphases of modern urban culture has been the quantification of human relationships and the reduction of human suffering to statistics. Only a few years after the *Journal of the Plague Year*, we must remember, Swift published *A Modest Proposal*. In Defoe's work the alternation of statistics and anecdotes reveals both a resistance to the purely analytical view and the feeling that it may be correct. For H. F. the view of human experience as divine is necessary to a recognition of the worth of others, the only counterbalance to the isolation and hostility encouraged by city life. His struggle to retain a spiritual conception of man is closely related to the conflicts in Defoe's novels, especially in *Roxana*, where Roxana's concern for maintaining economic independence threatens first to her daughter then to herself annihilation in a moral blackness Defoe could not fully contemplate. His perception of the conditions of urban life and his awareness of the moral situations in which they place the individual give the *Journal* immediacy to the modern reader, who—city dweller or suburbanite—lives with a constant sense of the impinging apocalyptic event, in suspicion and dread of his fellow man. This dimension of Defoe's work is reflected in much that we find in Camus' treatment of the qualities of modern life in *La Peste*. In each case, the life of the city under plague becomes paradigmatic for modern civilization. A comparison of the two works reveals the continuing vitality of Defoe's perceptions.

Chronology of Important Dates

1660	Daniel Foe born in London.
1665–66	The Great Plague.
1674–79 (?) (?)	Attended the school of Rev. Charles Morton at Newington Green, a village north of London, in preparation for the Presbyterian ministry.
1682–92	Engaged in various business ventures after deciding against entering the ministry. Captured by Algerian pirates off the coast of Holland, but soon released. Traveled widely in England and Europe. Published several political pamphlets.
1684	Married Mary Tuffley.
1692	Bankrupt for £17,000, result of wartime shipping losses.
1695	Name first appears as "Defoe."
1697–1701	Agent for William III in England and Scotland. Established brick and tile factory in Tilbury in 1697.
1701	*The True-Born Englishman*, a defense of William III.
1702	*The Shortest Way with the Dissenters*, an attack on the Church of England which led to imprisonment in Newgate the following year, a heavy fine, and sentence to stand in the pillory. Released with the help of Robert Harley, Tory Minister, for whom Defoe undertook intelligence and propaganda work until 1714. His brickworks failed in 1703.

1704	Began the *Review*, a journal of news and opinion.
1708	Moved from London to Stoke Newington, a northern suburb.
1713	Arrested for debt twice, probably at the instigation of political enemies.
1715–30	Served as political spy and propagandist for successive Whig ministries; actively promoted the Union of England and Scotland.
1715	*The Family Instructor.*
1719	*Robinson Crusoe.*
1720	*Captain Singleton.*
1722	*Moll Flanders, A Journal of the Plague Year, Colonel Jack.*
1724	*Roxana, A Tour thro' the Whole Island of Great Britain.*
1725	*The Complete English Tradesman.*
1731	Died April 24, in Ropemaker's Alley, hiding from creditors.

Notes on the Editor and Contributors

MAX BYRD, the editor of this volume in the Twentieth Century Views series, is Associate Professor of English at Yale University and the author of *Visits to Bedlam: Madness and Literature in the Eighteenth Century.*

BENJAMIN BOYCE, Professor of English Emeritus at Duke University, is also the author of two biographies: *The Benevolent Man: A Life of Ralph Allen of Bath* and *Tom Brown of Facetious Memory.*

W. AUSTIN FLANDERS is Associate Professor of English at the University of Pittsburgh.

J. PAUL HUNTER is Professor of English at Emory University. *The Reluctant Pilgrim: Defoe's Emblematic Method and the Quest for Form in Robinson Crusoe* appeared in 1966, and he has since written extensively on eighteenth-century literature.

MAXIMILLIAN E. NOVAK, Professor of English at UCLA, has written many studies of Defoe, notably *Economics and the Fiction of Daniel Defoe* and *Defoe and the Nature of Man*. He has also contributed to the California edition of the works of Dryden.

MARTIN PRICE is Professor of English at Yale. He is the author of *Swift's Rhetorical Art*, *To the Palace of Wisdom: Studies in Order and Energy from Dryden to Blake*, and one of the editors of the *Oxford Anthology of English Literature*.

MARK SCHORER is professor of English Emeritus at Berkeley. His books include *Sinclair Lewis* and *William Blake: The Politics of Vision*.

GEORGE A. STARR, Professor of English at Berkeley, the author of *Defoe and Spiritual Autobiography* and *Defoe and Casuistry*, has also edited *Moll Flanders* for the Oxford English Novels series.

JAMES R. SUTHERLAND is well-known for his volume on *English Literature of the Late Seventeenth Century* in the Oxford History of English Literature and a number of other books and essays. He is Professor of English Emeritus at the University of London.

DOROTHY VAN GHENT, late Professor of English at SUNY, Buffalo, wrote *The English Novel: Form and Function.*

IAN P. WATT, Professor of English at Stanford University, is the author of *The Rise of the Novel* as well as many essays on eighteenth-century literature.

VIRGINIA WOOLF is the famous novelist and critic.

Selected Bibliography

Texts

Three good editions are *Romances and Narratives*, ed. G. A. Aitken (London: J. M. Dent, 1895); *Works*, ed. G. H. Maynadier (Boston: D. Nickerson, 1903–4); *Novels and Selected Writings* (Oxford: Shakespeare Head Press, 1927–28). Most of the major fiction has recently been published in the Oxford English Novels series: two volumes, *Moll Flanders* (ed. George A. Starr) and *A Journal of the Plague Year* (ed. Louis A. Landa) have outstanding introductions and notes. A new edition of Defoe's works, under the direction of Maximillian E. Novak, is being undertaken by the University of Southern Illinois Press.

Defoe's *Letters*, ed. G. H. Healy (Oxford: Oxford University Press, 1955) chiefly concern his political activities. The *Review* has been edited by A. W. Secord (New York: Columbia University Press, 1938). Defoe's *Tour Thro' the Whole Island of Great Britain* is available complete, ed. G. D. H. Cole (London: Everyman's Library, 1927) and abridged, ed. Pat Rogers (Harmondsworth: Penguin Books, 1971).

Biographies

Moore, John Robert, *Daniel Defoe: Citizen of the Modern World.* Chicago: University of Chicago Press, 1958.

Sutherland, James R., *Defoe*. London: Methuen, 1937; 2nd. ed. 1950.

General

Baine, Rodney M., *Daniel Defoe and the Supernatural.* Athens: The University of Georgia Press, 1968.

Boulton, James T., "Daniel Defoe: His Language and Rhetoric," Introduction to *Daniel Defoe*, ed. James T. Boulton. New York: Schocken Books, 1965.

Braudy, Leo, "Daniel Defoe and The Anxieties of Autobiography," *Genre*, 6 (1973), 76–97.

Brown, Homer, "The Displaced Self in the Novels of Daniel Defoe," *ELH*, 38 (1971), 562–90.

Dobree, Bonamy, "Some Aspects of Defoe's Prose," in *Pope and His Contemporaries*, ed. James L. Clifford and Louis A. Landa. Oxford: Oxford University Press, 1949.

Donovan, Robert Alan, *The Shaping Vision: Imagination in the English Novel from Defoe to Dickens*. Ithaca: Cornell University Press, 1966.

Hunter, J. Paul, *The Reluctant Pilgrim: Defoe's Emblematic Method and Quest for Form in Robinson Crusoe*. Baltimore: The Johns Hopkins University Press, 1966.

McKillop, A. D., *Early Masters of English Fiction*. Lawrence, Kansas: University of Kansas Press, 1956.

Moore, John Robert, *Defoe in the Pillory and Other Studies*. Bloomington: Indiana University Press, 1939.

Novak, Maximillian E., *Defoe and the Nature of Man*. New York: Oxford University Press, 1963.

———, *The Economics and the Fiction of Daniel Defoe*. Berkeley and Los Angeles: University of California Press, 1962.

———, "Defoe's Theory of Fiction," *Studies in Philology*, 61 (1964), 650–68.

———, "The Problem of Necessity in Defoe's Fiction," *Philological Quarterly*, 40 (1961), 513–24.

Richetti, John, *Popular Fiction before Richardson*. Oxford: Oxford University Press, 1969.

Secord, A. W., *Studies in the Narrative Method of Defoe*. Urbana: University of Illinois Press, 1924.

Stamm, Rudolph, G., "Daniel Defoe: An Artist in the Puritan Tradition," *Philological Quarterly*, 15 (1936), 225–46.

Starr, George A., *Defoe and Casuistry*. Princeton: Princeton University Press, 1971.

——, *Defoe and Spiritual Autobiography*. Princeton: Princeton University Press, 1965.

——, "Defoe's Prose Style: 1. The Language of Interpretation," *Modern Philology*, 71 (1973–74), 277–94.

Sutherland, James R., *Defoe: A Critical Study*. Boston: Houghton Mifflin, 1971.

——, "The Relation of Defoe's Fiction to His Non-Fictional Writings," in *Imagined Worlds: Essays . . . in Honour of John Butt*, ed. Maynard Mack and Ian Gregor. London: Methuen, 1968.

Watt, Ian, *The Rise of the Novel: Studies in Defoe, Richardson and Fielding*. Berkeley and Los Angeles: University of California Press, 1957.

Zimmerman, Everett, *Defoe and the Novel*. Berkeley and Los Angeles: University of California Press, 1975.

Essays on Defoe's Major Fiction

ROBINSON CRUSOE

Ayres, Robert W., "Robinson Crusoe: 'Allusive Allegorick History,'" *PMLA*, 82 (1967), 399–407.

Ellis, Frank, ed., *Twentieth Century Interpretations of Robinson Crusoe*. Englewood Cliffs, N.J.: Prentice-Hall, 1969.

Hymer, Stephen, "Robinson Crusoe and Primitive Accumulation," *Monthly Review*, 23 (1971), 11–36.

MOLL FLANDERS

Brooks, Douglas, "Moll Flanders," *Essays in Criticism*, 19 (1969), 46–59.

Donoghue, Denis, "The Values of *Moll Flanders*," *Sewanee Review*, 71 (1963), 287–303.

Elliott, Robert C., ed., *Twentieth Century Interpretations of Moll Flanders.* Englewood Cliffs, N.J.: Prentice-Hall, 1970.

Novak, Maximillian E., "Defoe's Indifferent Monitor: The Complexity of *Moll Flanders*," *Eighteenth-Century Studies*, 3 (1970), 351–65.

Watt, Ian, "The Recent Critical Fortunes of *Moll Flanders*," *Eighteenth-Century Studies*, 1 (1967), 109–26.

ROXANA

Hume, Robert D., "The Conclusion of Defoe's *Roxana*: Fiasco or Tour de Force?" *Eighteenth-Century Studies*, 3 (1970), 475–90.

Novak, Maximillian E., "Crime and Punishment in Defoe's *Roxana*," *Journal of English and Germanic Philology*, 65 (1966), 445–65.

Petersen, Spiro, "The Matrimonial Theme of Defoe's *Roxana*," *PMLA*, 70 (1955), 166–91.

Starr, George A., "Sympathy v. Judgement in Roxana's First Liaison," in *The Augustan Milieu: Essays Presented to Louis A. Landa*, ed. Henry Knight Miller et al. Oxford: Oxford University Press, 1970.

A JOURNAL OF THE PLAGUE YEAR

Bastian, F., "Defoe's *Journal of the Plague Year* Reconsidered," *Review of English Studies*, N.S. 16 (1963), 151–73.

Schonhorn, Manuel, "Defoe's *Journal of the Plague Year:* Topography and Intention," *Review of English Studies*, 19 (1968), 387–402.

CAPTAIN SINGLETON

Scrimgeour, Gary J., "The Problem of Realism in Defoe's *Captain Singleton*," *Huntington Library Quarterly*, 27 (1963), 21–37.

COLONEL JACK

McBurney, William H., "Colonel Jacque: Defoe's Definition of the Complete Gentleman," *Studies in English Literature*, 2 (1962), 321–36.

TWENTIETH CENTURY VIEWS

British Authors

(continued on next page)

(continued from previous page)

TWENTIETH CENTURY VIEWS

American Authors

EDWARD ALBEE, edited by C. W. E. Bigsby (S-TC-125)
SHERWOOD ANDERSON, edited by Walter B. Rideout (S-TC-115)
AUDEN, edited by Monroe K. Spears (S-TC-38)
JAMES BALDWIN, edited by Keneth Kinnamon (S-TC-113)
SAUL BELLOW, edited by Earl Rovit (S-TC-122)
STEPHEN CRANE, edited by Maurice Bassan (S-TC-66)
E. E. CUMMINGS, edited by Norman Friedman (S-TC-98)
EMILY DICKINSON, edited by Richard B. Sewall (S-TC-28)
DOS PASSOS, edited by Andrew Hook (S-TC-114)
DREISER, edited by John Lydenberg (S-TC-96)
RALPH ELLISON, edited by John Hersey (S-TC-112)
EMERSON, edited by Milton R. Konvitz
  and Stephen E. Whicher (S-TC-12)
FAULKNER, edited by Robert Penn Warren (S-TC-65)
F. SCOTT FITZGERALD, edited by Arthur Mizener (S-TC-27)
ROBERT FROST, edited by James M. Cox (S-TC-3)
HAWTHORNE, edited by A. N. Kaul (S-TC-55)
HEMINGWAY, edited by Robert P. Weeks (S-TC-8)
HENRY JAMES, edited by Leon Edel (S-TC-34)
SINCLAIR LEWIS, edited by Mark Schorer (S-TC-6)
ROBERT LOWELL, edited by Thomas Parkinson (S-TC-79)
NORMAN MAILER, edited by Leo Braudy (S-TC-101)
BERNARD MALAMUD, edited by Leslie and Joyce Field (S-TC-123)
MELVILLE, edited by Richard Chase (S-TC-13)
ARTHUR MILLER, edited by Robert W. Corrigan (S-TC-84)
MODERN AMERICAN THEATER, edited by Alvin B. Kernan (S-TC-69)
MODERN BLACK NOVELISTS, edited by M. G. Cooke (S-TC-97)
MODERN BLACK POETS, edited by Donald B. Gibson (S-TC-106)
MARIANNE MOORE, edited by Charles Tomlinson (S-TC-86)
O'NEILL, edited by John Gassner (S-TC-39)
POE, edited by Robert Regan (S-TC-63)
EZRA POUND, edited by Walter Sutton (S-TC-29)

(continued on next page)

(continued from previous page)